TWELVE DAYS *in a* COMA

PASCAL MABIKA

Copyright © 2020 by Pascal Mabika

ISBN: Softcover   978-1-950596-61-4

All rights reserved. No part of this book may be reproduced or transmitted in any form or by any means, electronic or mechanical, including photocopying, recording, or by any information storage and retrieval system without express written permission from the author, except in the case of brief quotations embodied in critical reviews and certain other non-commercial uses permitted by copyright law.

Printed in the United States of America.

To order additional copies of this book, contact:
Bookwhip
1-855-339-3589
www.bookwhip.com

God is close by. However, by our frequent disobedience we wander away from him. In his immense love, he nevertheless keeps on talking to us through visions, dreams, and prophetic revelations.

CONTENTS

Preface 1
God is Here 7
My Stay in Senegal 12
Back to France 14
My Short Stay in Kigali, Rwanda 17
My Stay in Arusha 19
Life in Luxemburg 21
Life in Arusha 25
    At Work 26
    Involvement in Ministry 26
    Life as a Couple 29
Trip to the Holy Land 30
During the Coma 35
Out of Coma 37
    Do Not Tease God in His Sanctuary! 37
    Why Must We Flee from Sin? 38
        Dancing 39
        How can dancing insidiously affect a blessing? 41
How Do We Tease God? 42
    1. In Our Studies 42
    2. At Our Workplaces 42
    3. Within the Couple and the Family 44
    4. In Christian Communities 45

    How to Fear God?..48
    How Do We Defile the Temple of God?....................................48
    We Fear God by Avoiding Vain Wrangling...............................49
Medical Evacuation...52
Conclusion..53

PREFACE

In the Bible, each time God performed a miracle, his servants marked such an event by a sign or a monument. When Jacob met the angel of the Lord, for instance, at the end of that divine encounter, he erected a stone into a monument at that spot.

My family and I would like to do the same. Through these pages, we wish to testify about the miracle we witnessed in Israel. By so doing, we hope to make it a memorable experience for anyone who wishes to know what God did for me and for my family as a whole. I believe this victory also belongs to the church of God, and I pray that this testimony will transform nations, this generation, even generations to come, why not?

Thanks to the experience I share in this book, I believe God added more days to my life, and he did so for a reason. This new lease of life is a gift I cannot afford to take light heartedly, and just shove into a drawer as if it was a cheap toy. That is why from the moment I came back to life, I never stopped thinking of how best I could express my gratitude to God and all who stood by me through this horrifying experience. From deep within, I felt the urge to record the wonderful work that God accomplished: *my resurrection*. This is a privilege I wish to share with everyone created by God, so as to edify everyone and above all to confirm that God is right here on Planet Earth. I have the inner conviction that by putting this testimony in writing, I will reach out to many more people, beginning from my immediate neighbours, my country and the entire Church.

Through this book, it is my honor to express my utmost and unspeakable gratitude to the following persons:

- My wife, who displayed unparalleled courage in bearing the burden of a lifeless body for twelve days, and took care of me spiritually and physically;
- My four daughters—Eunice, Diyenat, Maud, and Capucine Mabika—who believed their mother and stood by her in fasting and prayer. They followed her every step as the Lord guided her during those moments of trial. They also displayed the faith in God that their mother and I had taught them from their early childhood;
- The senior officials of the International Criminal Tribunal for Rwanda (ICTR), my employer, notably Mr. Adama Dieng, then assistant secretary-general and ICTR registrar; Ms. Sarah Kilemi, chief of administration; and Dr. Hernandez Epée, for their unwavering administrative and medical support ;
- My in-laws in Congo-Brazzaville, France, Canada, and the United States of America, Uncles Levy, Assollant, Ben, Auntie Vicky and their families, and especially my wife's brothers and sisters, who stood with me spiritually and materially—Daptone and Delphine MBouyou in particular, who honoured us by their presence at the thanksgiving ceremony in Arusha, Tanzania, on 25 June 2011; Claire Mabika, Brez, Pussy (Dr. Birangui), whose professional and medical support facilitated my evacuation from Israel to France; my kid brothers—Hortense Mpassi, Chantal et Axel Mayenne, Yvette Mabirou, Jeanine et Jean-Pierre Moukala—for their prayers and support;
- My sole sister, Josephine Matamba, and my niece Christelle Moukabi, who assisted us morally and materially;
- My church in Arusha, especially my pastor and his wife, Charles and Judith Akwera, who, alongside Kenneth and Edith, beloved brethren in Christ, organised fasting and prayer for us. They

called several times while we were in Israel just to know how I was faring;
- The men and women of God whom God brought our way and who just fell in love with us and gave us their total support throughout this ordeal. May I mention in particular Bishop John and Apostle Trice Shumbusho, who fasted and prayed for us and who, with their church, took active part in the organisation and the eventual success of the above-mentioned thanksgiving ceremony; with unwavering assistance of Chantal and her husband, Leon; I will not forget Pastor Balthazar and his church, Bethel Church in Sokoine 1, Arusha, for their spiritual support;
- Our brothers and sisters of ICTR Christian Fellowship, led by Pastor Randolph Tebbs. Here, let me mention our beloved Debra Tulcidas, who unrelentingly comforted and encouraged my wife by her words and deeds, all rooted in the Word of God; Tolu and Georges Olowoye, who kept on reminding us of God's prophecies they had witnessed about us; Mama Stella Karumuna and Mama Jennifer Kahurananga and their husbands, the men's fellowship at ICTR, led by Brother Eugene Tawe;
- Our home prayer cell, whose members and entire families threw in unflinching spiritual support —Irma and Gloria Adjete, Margaret Mwaura, Doreen Maina, Pastors Evelyn and Randolph Tebbs, Debra Tulcidas, Alphonse and Rachel Van, Forias and Renifa Madenga, among others;
- How dare I forget our friends, our spiritual parents and mentors within the framework of Family Life Ministry, which we coordinate in Arusha, namely David and Jayne Mutiga, Kirabo and Mary Lukwago, Reverend Ken and Joy Kimiywe of Nairobi Pentecostal Church, Valley Road, for their fervent prayers and earnest fasting;
- The respective churches of our four children, and those of my senior and junior siblings, especially our friend prophetess

Maggie in the United States, who did her utmost best to connect us to a local church in Israel;
- Prophet Kolbeinn of Iceland and Pastor Sylvain. The Lord had used this prophet mightily in March 2010 to speak to us. He had uttered a prophecy that has come true today;
- Permit me to express sincere gratitude to my brothers and kinsmen, Nathalie and Auguste Biyo, Maryse and Serge Mbounda, Judith and Marcel Ngoma-Mouaya, Maria and Moussounga Itsouhou Mbadinga, for their immense support;

I am grateful to God who brought certain men and women along our pathway as a family and used these persons amazingly to pull us through the terrible moments we witnessed faraway in Israel. I am referring to Ambassador Jacob; his wife; Bruria, his mother-in-law; the director of the travel agency in Israel, Vered Hasharon Tour, who organised our guided visit there; Danny, and his entire team, especially Charity, for their professionalism, but above all, good heart and divine help, as well as the Assembly of God church beautifully located on a hill in Haifa.

I carry deep gratitude and profound respect for the staff of Rambam Hospital in Haifa, especially towards the eminent neurosurgeon, Dr Amsalem, who did the surgery and took total care of me; Dr Mayo who accompanied me during my medical evacuation from Israel to Paris; and the nurses and other paramedics at the intensive care unit for displaying great professionalism.

I do not forget the doctors and staff of the neurosurgery unit in the Bretonneau Hospital in Tours, France, which took me in for further treatment upon arrival from Israel. My special thoughts go to my physiotherapist, who patiently re-educated and helped me to walk again; my two speech therapists, Dr. Maryvonne Fourtouil and Dr. Valérie Legrand, who worked hard in training me so as to reboot my memory.

Let me also thank all who stood with us in prayer, be it from close quarters or from distant locations, or who contributed in producing this book. Permit me to particularly mention Kevin, my nephew in Lille, who was introduced to me by Josephine, my kid sister, and whom God endowed with the commitment and strength to type these pages; my brother in Christ Aatsa Atogho, who was available to interpret into English all I had to say each time I had to tell my story and especially during the thanksgiving ceremony organised by my family on 25 June 2011, at Corridor Springs Hotel, in Arusha, Tanzania. On that day, before an audience of nearly two hundred guests from the Christian community of Arusha, including church elders, pastors, and bishops, as well as some Muslim friends, we gave thanks and praises to God. Aatsa also translated this book from its original French version into English.

May you all be richly blessed in Jesus's name!

GOD IS HERE

"Lord, why was I born fatherless?" I queried God. I was stretched out in my bed, in the midst of anguish, eyes staring at the ceiling of my bedroom.

I got the answer to my question in a manner I least expected. All of a sudden I saw the film of my childhood unfolding before me, portraying how much God had taken care of me. During all the months I was in my mother's womb, I was in the palm of his hand. Three months into this pregnancy, my mother became a widow.

In my bed, I uttered the following prayer: "Lord, I thank you for granting me to be born in a family of kind-hearted people. In addition, you watched over me during my entire childhood, enabling me to grow and keeping me alive up till this day. I thank you for your benefits. But Lord, why did you do all this? Was it for me to end up a mere onlooker down here?" After that simple prayer, I fell asleep.

Let me tell you about myself.

I was born on 7 February 1952, in a village called N'zambi-kalla, Congo-Brazzaville. My mother lost her husband when she was three months pregnant. God arranged things in such a way that my mother would have all her relatives around her. All those who knew her late husband, my father, loved and respected her deeply. It is in that environment that God gave me life and was born.

Mum raised me within her family whom she had resorted to during her widowhood. She remained a widow for six years before she remarried. She was a fervent Christian and a deaconess in her church. In 1958, I started my education at the government school in Divenié. I was six years old at the time. Sometime later, Mum took ill and handed me over to Elizabeth Moukabi, her elder sister, a Catholic by faith. Consequently, I had to move from the government to the Catholic school, close to our home.

From class 1 to class 3 primary school, I received Catholic education. While in class 3, Germain Mangou, my paternal uncle, died in Pointe-Noire and my aunt, now a widow, decided to take me back to my mother, who had remarried in Dolisie and had already given birth to my kid sister, Josephine Matamba.

In Dolisie, my mother enrolled me in St Joseph's School, which I attended until class 6 when I passed the common entrance examination into secondary school and also obtained my first school leaving certificate in 1964. That is when I began facing the problem of finding a place in a secondary school of general education in Dolisie, in the Niari region. Once again, I was compelled to move far away from my parents to pursue my secondary education in the newly created Divénié College. I was there until form 2. In moving to form 3, I found a place in Dolisie secondary. In form 4, I did very well in the BEPC, the equivalent of the ordinary-level general certificate of education (GCE). From there, I moved to Pointe-Noire, the economic capital of Congo-Brazzaville to study at Victor Augagneur High School. It was in this town that I received Jesus Christ as my personal Lord and Savior and got myself baptised one Pentecost Day by Rev. Pastor N'Doundou, a renowned Congolese gospel preacher. Shortly thereafter, I joined the Evangelical Scripture Union in order to study the Bible and eventually serve God as other young Christians.

In upper sixth form, I passed my advanced-level certificate in the sciences and boarded the train to Brazzaville, the political capital of Congo-Brazzaville. I enrolled in my first year at the faculty of sciences, biochemistry department, specialization in biology. While at the university, sometime between 1974 and 1975, I joined the University Scripture Union. It was during this period that I met Leontine Birangui, a Christian and a student in the faculty of letters, who later became my wife. How I bless God for that day!

I passed the examination in biology and health sciences with flying colours and earned a cooperation and assistance scholarship (FAC) and left for further studies at the Pasteur Institute in Lyons, France. There I obtained my diploma in laboratory health sciences and picked up a job at the Regional Centre for Blood Transfusion. As for Leontine, she also got a Congolese government scholarship to study at the School of Translators, Interpreters and Foreign Trade Managers in Lille.

On 26 July 1980, Léontine and I got married in Lille, a union that has flourished to see the birth of four beautiful girls, namely, Eunice, Diyenat, Maud, and Capucine. Six months after Capucine was born, my wife found a job in Senegal, further to a written test and an interview. To allow her report for duty that was to begin with a six-month probation, I accepted to stay and take care of our four children. At the time, I was in second-year architecture student and was a temporal staff at an employment agency known as Manpower. Besides these occupations, I had to take care of our four girls. Six months later, we joined her in Senegal, where I quickly enrolled in third year architecture at the Dakar School of Architecture and Town Planning. When I got to sixth year, without giving us the opportunity to graduate, this school was shut down.

As a result, I was forced to return to France where I was admitted into fifth year architecture. In 1993, the entire family joined me in France, after the African Centre for Monetary Studies, where my wife worked at in Senegal, laid off its staff for restructuring purposes. Shortly after that, my wife left for the United States. She worked for the Embassy of the Republic of the Congo in Washington, DC. All the while, I lived alone with our four daughters, watching over them day and night, with the help of the Lord and in fellowship with him. To get my daughters to love prayer and serve the Lord, I kept them occupied with musical-instruments lessons, mainly piano and flute. Generally, at the end of each day, we would have a mini musical concert at home; they would play the hymns they had learnt on their musical instruments, while I accompanied them with my guitar. It was a small but a beautiful choir. My children composed tunes that they got to play in churches in France and in America. They even composed a song that they sang to welcome their mother in France when she came for vacation. It was thanks to all that practice and time spent together that my daughters and I easily joined the church led by Pastor Bongo in his early days. There, it was our daughter Maud who played the piano during praise and worship sessions.

Once again, I wish to thank the Lord for those moments when singlehandedly I had to take care of our four daughters while my wife was working at the African Centre for Monetary Studies (ACMS) in Senegal. I became the laughingstock of some friends and relatives who could not understand how I could have allowed my wife to work so far away from home. I saw the hand of God back me in this uncommon and difficult situation. He granted me a special capacity to organize myself such that by reading the Word of God together and trying to understand it, I raised our daughters in a disciplined manner. I urged them to sing hymns and other Christian songs as well as get involved in musical activities. At the same time, I was studying architecture in Lille. During a one-day study trip to Paris, I do recall that due to a huge traffic jam, I got back so late that I was unable to pick up our four girls from school. The Lord stepped in and got the headmistress of the nursery, Ms. Gressier, to take all four girls to her home. That does not happen often in France, you know. When I got back, she reassured me that the children were at her home and I could go fetch them. I will never thank God enough for his protection and such grace. Blessed be his holy name!

Furthermore, while I was at the School of Architecture in Lille, France, and my wife was in Senegal, I had a weekend job. During the week, whenever I took my children to the day care or the nursery school, they were always very neat and well behaved. This left the nursery teachers astonished and full of admiration towards the single man that

I was, taking care of very young children between six months and six years of age. From time to time, they would encourage me and name me as an example to be emulated by other men, family heads who also had children in the same school. In that situation, the Lord helped me out abundantly. He granted me the will and the strength to take good care of our children while pursuing my studies at the School of Architecture. My reward came in the form of success into third year architecture.

Meanwhile, my wife was confirmed in her position in Dakar, Senegal. With that appointment, and from an administrative point of view, she could get us to join her in Dakar. And that is just what happened in July 1987.

MY STAY IN SENEGAL

As soon we dropped our bags in Senegal, I enrolled at the School of Architecture and Town Planning of Dakar. My wife and I joined the Protestant church in Senegal. In a short time, I was co-opted as the mentor of the youth group. I joined the choir and the Bible Study Group in the church. I became part of the technical committee in charge of managing church buildings and property, led by a Cameroonian architect. The property comprised the church buildings, the Protestant school, as well as the Liberty Centre, which hosted training and sociocultural activities of the church. I renovated it. From time to time, the architect and I alternated in leading church services.

Before long, the elders appointed me as a member of the Council of Wisemen, called upon to assist the pastor administratively and spiritually in tasks such as staff recruitment, paying church-related bills, organizing Bible study sessions, prayer meetings, and pastoral visits to the flock.

In all this, I could see God's hand at work in my life. In all I undertook, I could feel his presence. My studies were going on very well, my children were happy, and my wife was doing great in her work as translator-interpreter. She was also very active in church activities. As the leader of the Women's Group, she traveled abroad to represent the church at regional Christian conferences. As a family, our stay in Dakar was showered with blessings, for God was and still is (thank God!) with us, as stated in Psalms 91:1–5:

> He who dwells in the shelter of the Most high, will rest in the shadow of the Almighty,
> I will say of the Lord, "He is my refuge and my fortress, my God in whom I trust";
> Surely He will save you from the fowler's snare and from the deadly pestilence.
> He will cover you with His feathers, and under his wings you will find refuge;
> His faithfulness will be your shield and rampart.
> You will not fear the terror of night, nor the arrow that flies by midday, nor the pestilence that stalks in the darkness,
> Nor the plague that destroys at midday.
>
> Psalms 91:1–5

Reassured by this Word of God, I worked as hard I could to improve my performance at school. I do recall that we were obliged to return to France six years later when my wife lost her job due to restructuring of the African Centre for Monetary Studies, her employer, and though I had not yet defended my end-of-course thesis. During the trying moments that followed, we stood on God's Word, in Psalms 23:1, 4: "The Lord is my Shepherd, I shall be in want…Even though I walk through the valley of the shadow of death, I will fear no evil, for you are with me; your rod and your staff, they comfort me" (NIV).

BACK TO FRANCE

I thank the Lord who, six years earlier on, had led me to keep the keys of the apartment in which we lived before leaving for Senegal. I had handed it to a Senegalese friend, also studying at the same school, to continue paying the rents. It was also in a bid to help him pursue his studies comfortably. So upon our return, we went back to our apartment in Lille. The children were enrolled at Triolo College, and life as a family was rebuilt, thanks to God Almighty. Deep inside me, I was pleading for God's intervention. It was difficult to see my wife sitting there unemployed, while I was still at the School of Architecture in Lille, as I had not yet gotten the opportunity to defend my end-of-year thesis.

God heard my prayer. A few weeks later, in October 1993 precisely, my wife obtained short-term contracts as a consultant with the United Nations Development Fund for Women (UNIFEM) and the World Bank.

Afterwards, my wife left for the United States to visit her kid sister, Rose Christiane, today deceased, who was married to an American and had two children, Taina and Junior. She lived in Secaucus, in New Jersey. A month later, she met the Congolese ambassador in Washington, DC, and the latter told her that the embassy requires her services as a translator-interpreter. This is how she was offered a position in the Congolese embassy. One more time, God was at work in our lives. Blessed be his holy name!

Once again, I was all by myself in Lille with our girls, who had grown into teenagers. Armed with the same courage and buoyed by the same faith in God, we organized ourselves to lead before God-balanced academic, social, and spiritual lives. During the holidays, we would join my wife, who had settled in a big and beautiful apartment in Silver Spring, Maryland, from where she was able to do her work at the embassy. She had joined Bethel World Outreach Church, which she discovered thanks to a diplomat from Niger who worshipped there. She had met him miraculously at one of her official functions. She began serving the Lord in that church as interpreter for French. Since there was a huge French-speaking population in the church, by so doing, she met a great need. She would interpret simultaneously every sermon by the resident pastor, Bishop Darlington Johnson, or any other minister who came along.

On the first Sunday my wife introduced us as her family to the congregation, the bishop asked our daughters to show what they could do with their flutes. By the ensuing performance, they demonstrated their mastery of their instruments. They went on to sing a song they composed and left the entire assembly amazed. There was a rapturous applause by the audience. What an encouragement for our daughters! From that day, each time we came on holidays, the first thing they would be asked to do was to perform, be it in Bethel or other venues where such events were organized.

Though we traveled a lot, our relationship with the Lord never waned. Much to the contrary, these movements only strengthened our faith that we shared in many Christian assemblies whenever the opportunity arose. This is what the Bible says in Psalm 1:1–3:

> Blessed is the man who walks not in the counsel of the wicked, nor stands in the way of the sinners, nor sits in the seat of scoffers; but his delight is in the law of the Lord, and on his law he meditates day and night. He is like a tree planted by streams of water, that yields its fruit in its season, and its leaf does not wither. In all that he does, he prospers.
>
> Psalm 1:1–3

As long as we abide in Christ who is the stream that refreshes us morning, afternoon, and evening, we remain "fertilized" under the Holy Spirit.

My wife was in the United States until 1 October 1 1995. On third of October, she was recruited by the United Nations System for a peacekeeping mission in Luanda, Angola, known as UNAVEM III, or United Nations Angola Verification Mission. None other than God could have made this possible. She has written elaborately about this miraculous recruitment in the book she will soon publish as the testimony of her life under the title *Testimonies*.

This UN contract, for which we remain abundantly grateful to God, brought a great change to our living standards as a family. Our last three daughters were able to attend the American School in Switzerland (TASIS), in Lugano, Switzerland, one of the best American schools abroad. They studied there while in boarding school, one after the other, until they moved on to university in the United States. In the meantime, Eunice, our eldest daughter, who had remained with me in Lille, passed her international baccalaureate, along with Afi, the daughter of a Togolese man who worked with my wife, but who today, sad to say, is of late. Afi, to whom I was a guardian, went to a university in London, while our daughter went to a university in Evansville, Indiana. This American university granted her a scholarship.

My wife, I, and our other three daughters accompanied Eunice on commencement day at Evansville University. There, and for the first time, we met a Congolese family (father, mother, and two children) that had settled there. They received us very warmly and facilitated our task in settling our daughter at the university, while the father became our daughter's guardian in that town. May God bless them even more! In that family, we saw God's hand powerfully outstretched to take care of us and our daughter in particular, a young French girl studying in the United States.

Here again, we see how at every stage God stepped in to make things easy. We thank him for all these persons whom he led to us and who have been amazingly at our disposal.

MY SHORT STAY IN KIGALI, RWANDA

In 1997, when my wife returned from the United Nations Verification Mission in Angola (UNAVEM), we left Lille for Rwanda, where she had found another job with the UN International Criminal Tribunal for Rwanda, based in Kigali. A year later, my wife and I got our girls enrolled in TASIS, from where they would learn English and be able to follow the American system of Education. After we got back to Lille from the United States, I drove the three other girls to TASIS, their school in Lugano, Switzerland, while my wife returned to her job in Kigali. The journey was a long 900 km drive, via Belgium, Luxemburg, and Germany. It is worthwhile to mention that I covered this distance every holiday period—at Christmas, Easter and in summer—to pick them up whenever school broke up and to drop them off whenever it reopened. I knew the way so well I could drive there with my eyes closed! I thank the Lord who on each of these occasions watched over us. Not once did we have an accident.

From Kigali, I returned to France to continue with work and school. It was not easy. I experienced trying times as jobs were hard to come by. I had to resort to holding part-time positions in Lille, Paris, and Luxemburg. I had therefore to give up the three-bedroom apartment I was occupying in Lille as I was now living alone. A real ordeal! The Lord was still with me. I kept courage and did not lose heart. In the meantime, in September 2002, my wife was posted at the ICTR office, based in Arusha, Tanzania. With all the children now away from home, one in the United States and the other three in a boarding school in

Switzerland, I joined her there. I spent many months at home while hunting for a job. My efforts were futile.

I therefore returned to France. After further search initiatives, I found a job with a company called Securitas in Paris. There within my team I met a colleague who was also a pastor. Oftentimes, during our conversations, he would ask after my family and particularly about my wife who was all the way in Africa. It was during one of our conversations that he made me understand that it was not healthy for me to live far away from my wife and that regardless of what it would take, I had to join her and live with her. I heeded his advice since his words of encouragement were backed by the Word of God.

MY STAY IN ARUSHA

With all our girls having left for further studies in the United States, I traveled back to Tanzania to join my spouse. God looked upon me favourably. I met an American architect who was looking for an assistant to help him with the architectural design of a hospital in 3D. I went to see him, and with my computer, I did a presentation on what I could do. He gave me the blueprints of his project and asked me to reproduce it overnight. The next day, I submitted my results. He was amazed. That very moment, he offered me a one-year contract for the construction of a hospital in Arusha known as Selian Hospital. I worked relentlessly on this project until the work site was opened. This hospital was constructed, strictly following my architectural orientations and instructions, and today it is fully operational. Of course, I am proud of its architecture.

I thank the Lord, who once more moved in my life by giving me the opportunity to contribute to this project while I was by my wife, who was already employed at the United Nations International Criminal Tribunal for Rwanda. We lived together for about a year, worshiping together at Bethel Church, Tanzania branch. I have kept a good relationship with the American architect.

I thank the Lord who granted me the opportunity to grow spiritually within the various churches where I worshipped as we moved from one country to the other, either for academic or for professional reasons. I am hereby referring to the Evangelical church in Congo-Brazzaville, my fatherland; the Protestant church in Senegal; the Evangelical church in Lille, and the Reformed church in Thionville, both in France; Bethel

World Outreach Ministry International in Maryland, USA; Shining Light Church in Kigali, Rwanda; and Dominion Restoration Church in Arusha, Tanzania. I will be remiss not to mention the various Christian fellowships I attended and sometimes led, such as ICTR Christian Fellowship, ICTR Men's Fellowship, the home fellowship my wife and I started in our home in 2002 and would meet every Thursday till date, the home cell group hosted by Alphonse and Rachel Van, our brethren in Christ from Cote d'Ivoire and Tanzania, and the prayer group led by our dear friends, Pastors Randolph and Evelyn Tebbs from Liberia.

Over and above all, the ministries the Lord has entrusted to my wife and I have enabled us to grow in our walk with him, to know him better and in a concrete manner, and to learn to depend on him when it comes to preparing and executing planned events. These are the Family Life Ministry and the Youth Ministry that I would mention further down in more details.

Once the hospital project was over, my wife and I returned to France on annual leave. Again, the Lord was good to me. I got a job drawing digital designs for building plans for banks and other office buildings in Luxemburg. So while my wife was heading back to Arusha, I stayed in Luxemburg.

LIFE IN LUXEMBURG

In Luxemburg, the job offer I received was from JB-Interlux, an architectural firm led by a Congolese who happened to be a brother-in-law of mine. He hosted me for about four months while we worked together at the firm, digitalizing architectural plans of buildings. My brother-in-law, his wife, and their two little boys were so generous; such generosity could only have been a gift from God. For all they did for me, may God reward them a hundredfold! I then found a three-bedroom apartment in Thionville, France, close to Luxemburg, the capital city, where lodging was very expensive. I opted to live in France, go to work in Luxemburg by train every morning, and return every evening, like many French do. After all, commuting was easy, given that trains were many and punctual.

In Thionville, my apartment was well located on the third floor of a building, above a bank and opposite a shopping centre in town, surrounded by all you would need, such as a grocery, a pharmacy, bus stops, and other facilities, right under the building. I thanked the Lord very much for it.

I began worshipping at the Reformed Church in France, which was located next to the main square. Initially, I called the pastor by telephone and took an appointment. Two days later, we met at 2:00 p.m. after I left work. The pastor asked me, "What can you do?" I told him, "I can sing and lead Bible studies." He introduced me to the Bible studies coordinator, an elder in the church named Claude. The latter handed to me the Bible study program, which fortunately was convenient for me. Consequently, I started attending Bible study meetings, during which I introduced the opening-prayer slot. When Claude noticed how active

I was during these sessions, he asked me to take over the leadership of the Bible study meetings.

During the Christmas holidays, my wife and children joined me in Thionville. I introduced them to the pastor and all the members of the Bible study group. On account of their active participation, the pastor and my family came up with the idea of organizing an evening for praise and worship. This praise-and-worship evening, organized by our girls and their cousins, who had formed a musical group called Ze Family, brought a great band led by Christophe on stage. Those who came with their musical instruments to support the children were Pastor Philippe himself on the drums, Claude on the bass guitar, as well as many other family members, uncles, and aunties from other towns in France. It was a great success. The members of the audience marveled. The church congregation was pleased. That evening had such a great impact that it made headlines in the church's newsletter.

After the concert, we invited everyone present, i.e. singers, musicians, and family members, for dinner in our apartment. It was on that occasion that my family and I got to know Prophet Pierre who led us in thanksgiving immediately after our dinner and had since become one of our best friends and spiritual mentors, as well as his wife, Laurence. You could feel the presence of God that night. It was a memorable evening.

I continued working in Luxemburg, and on some Sundays, I would join my brother-in-law and his family and worship at their church, the Italian Christian Community in Luxemburg. Unknown to me, the first time I went there, the Lord had a surprise for me. I knew nobody there at the time. On that day, I was sitting alone at the back of the hall where the service was taking place. I was reading my Bible when someone patted me on the shoulder. Taken unawares, I turned around to find that it was the pastor of the church who had just come in through a door located behind my seat. He told me, "Brother, the Lord told me that today you are the one to minister to us through the Word." It was difficult to conceal my surprise. I replied by saying, "With pleasure,

Pastor!" At that very moment, the Spirit reminded me that a child of God should be ready at all times!

After the usual introduction to the brethren, when the time came, I preached from Psalm 23 starting with, "The Lord is my Shepherd, I shall not want." The congregation, including my brother-in-law and his family, who had come in shortly before I began speaking, was touched by the message. From that day on, the pastor would request me to lead prayer meetings in the church in Luxemburg whenever I could go there.

In addition, I was taken aback when some brethren in Luxemburg, who had happened to know that I had moved into an empty apartment in Thionville, had taken upon themselves to pool efforts to furnish it. They brought kitchen utensils, from the cooker to the refrigerator, including the crockery holder with all the crockery, pots, bed sheets, bed covers, you name it—and all these items were virtually new! I was at a loss for words to express my deep gratitude and how touched I felt by such a gesture—a gesture that is very rare in Europe of all places! Through that experience, I saw God working once more as my provider. My heart burst out and flowed towards him in spontaneous thanksgiving. True to the topic of my sermon, he had demonstrated that he was indeed my Shepherd and that I was never going to lack anything.

I will never forget the look on my wife's and daughters' faces the first time they walked into that apartment upon their arrival in Thionville some months down the road. It was Christmas time, and they were to make preparations for the Christian concert mentioned above. They could not believe their eyes. Everything we needed to enable us to live together there was available.

After the Ze Family concert in Thionville, my famiy and I decided to open our apartment to all those who were ready to join us in prayer. That was how our home became a place of prayer every Friday evening for our neighbors, the brethren from the Reformed church, Claude, Christophe, his wife, and Prophet Pierre Spataro. For more than two years, even after my wife and children returned to Tanzania and America for work or further studies, we met and prayed on a regular basis. This notwithstanding, I continued leading Bible study every Tuesday evening at the Reformed church in Thionville.

That was my life in Thionville and Luxemburg—a life consecrated to Jesus Christ as much as possible. I thank the Lord for the times when, during those prayer meetings, he reached out and saved souls, encouraged and lifted up the broken-hearted, delivered many from sinful habits, and provided for the needs of many others.

And yet, I faced serious challenges. The company in Luxemburg was facing difficulties in paying its workers because its clients took very long to pay honorarium they owed in return for its services. These were banks and other companies in Luxemburg, the capital city, as well as in other countries. I ended up working without a dime for six months with my brother-in-law, in the hope that once money came in and things fell into place, I would get my salary as promised. As a consequence, my bills for unpaid rents continued to rise, as well as that for basic utilities and housing taxes. Eventually, and in order to stop the situation from going out of hand, I decided to quit the apartment and look for another job in Paris. Thank God, the brethren in Thionville offered to store all my property in the church premises free of charge! Claude helped me actively as I moved house and took care of all my personal belongings. This was work he had done himself one time, along with our first daughter, Eunice, who had come from Dublin, Ireland, where she was working, just to help! May God bless the work of their hands!

In this new situation, I prayed for God's intervention. And without delay, he answered me.

It was from Luxemburg that I got a call from the United Nations International Criminal Tribunal for Rwanda. Sequel to an interview for a job application filed many years ago, I was offered a contract in the Witness and Victims Services Section (WVSS) of the tribunal. How grateful I was to God for that phone call!

After concerting with my wife, I decided to join her. Thus, I started work at the WVSS. We thanked the Lord for his grace that had reunited us once again, while our children were doing well in good schools in America and Switzerland.

LIFE IN ARUSHA

We had asked the Lord to make our home a place of prayer and worship. The Lord led us to devote Thursday evenings for this ministry. Basically, we would invite brothers and sisters in Christ, especially those who today are members of our prayer group (home fellowship) and many others to join us. We would study the Word of God, share it, and praise God together, and at the end of each session, we would have some refreshments or a light meal before parting company. The Lord has done so many great things for us and among us that we will never cease thanking him. Until this day, every Thursday evening, this prayer group still meets in our home.

In addition to this home fellowship, my wife and I are committed in serving the Lord within our church known as Dominion Restoration Church, led by Pastor Charles Akwera, our spiritual father, and his charming wife, Judith, affectionately known as Mama Muchungaji in Kiswahili, or simply Mama Pastor. They have a very pretty daughter called Glory, a gift from God. My wife and I are among the elders of the church. Apart from being one of the ministers of praise and worship, she is also in charge of the youth department in the church. As for me, I am in charge of protocol (the ushers), and virtually, every Sunday, I stand at the door of the church and welcome the people to the worship service. I am also in charge of maintaining discipline after Sunday school to stop any loitering during the service and ensure that it is quiet and peaceful during worship. As part of our church responsibilities, my wife and I are often called upon to counsel young people, married and unmarried, to sensitize them and help them make the right decisions, such as choosing a partner, running their homes, or managing their professional careers.

At Work

Here, God granted me favor before my immediate boss. Once she realized that I had good computer skills and would readily assist colleagues who were yet unfamiliar with the tool, she appointed me in charge of the pilot project of digitalizing the archives of the tribunal. Endowed with wisdom and intelligence from the Lord, I put in place the principles and modalities for implementing the pilot project. My boss was so amazed she eventually entrusted me with the responsibility of training all who were newly recruited into our section. I ended up training twenty-three new colleagues, an achievement that earned me great appreciation from my hierarchical superiors. I was confirmed as the head of the group. Colleagues would consult me each time they ran into a difficulty. I would do my utmost to help them. Thanks to the Lord, who had granted me the skills and the enabling for this task, I was available to help. Through these professional activities, I ushered in an atmosphere of trust and respect in the section and among colleagues. As much as possible, I tried to apply the divine principle of loving my neighbor as myself.

Involvement in Ministry

My wife and I joined the prayer group of the UN ICTR, known as ICTR Christian Fellowship, created in 1996. The current coordinator is Pastor Randolph Tebbs, a brother from Liberia, who is also a UN civil servant. He is ably supported in this office by his wife, Pastor Evelyn Tebbs. We meet every work day except Friday from 1:00 p.m. to 2 pm. This group, which is made up of Christians from the tribunal, the East African Community, and brethren from the town of Arusha, meets to praise and worship God, intercede for the nations and particularly for Tanzania, for their employers and employees, and for their family and individual needs. The founder and spiritual father of this fellowship is Bishop John Shumbusho, a UN civil servant too. Many pastors and evangelists from neighboring churches join us. The Lord has accomplished many great miracles and transformed many lives within this group.

Concurrently, the Lord has granted my wife and me a burden for two other ministries that we are coordinating in Arusha—the family life ministry and the youth ministry in the town of Arusha. As for the family life ministry, it was started as a branch in Arusha by Alex and Kate Aboagye, a Ghanaian couple. When, for professional reasons, they settled in the Hague in the Netherlands, they entrusted its coordination to my wife and me. The family life ministry sets out to build and strengthen the family unit, through national and international seminars organized annually by its executive committee on topics dealing with life within the couple, parenting, parent-child relations, celibacy, marriage and divorce, widowhood, and managing a home financially, all grounded on the Word of God. We believe that strong families make strong churches, strong churches make strong communities, and strong communities make strong nations.

About two hundred people attend these seminars. They come from Kenya, Uganda, Rwanda, Burundi, Democratic Republic of Congo, Tanzania, the Netherlands, as well as from the United Nations community. The main speakers at these seminars are men and women of God who are knowledgeable in family matters and counseling and rich in experience. These are Rev. Ken Kimiywe and his wife, Joy, the senior pastor of the Nairobi Pentecostal Church, Valley Road; David and Jayne Mutiga, engineer and associate professor at the Nairobi University respectively; Kirabo and Mary Lukwago, proprietors of the New Day Gospel Bookshop in Nairobi; the Bensons; David and Margaret Gacanja, marriage counselors in Nairobi, Kenya.

Concerning the executive committee of the family life that my wife and I are heading, it is made up as follows: Pastors Randolph and Evelyn Tebbs, Pastor Stephen and Mary Owino, Jennifer Karegyesa,

Beth Luzuka, Pastor Robert and his spouse Christine, Pastor Philip and his spouse, as well as my wife and I. My wife usually plays the role of master of ceremony during these seminars.

As regards the youth ministry in Arusha, which the Lord revealed to my wife through his Word way back on 22 May 2010, during a mission in Kigali, Rwanda, it started with a small seminar organized for unmarried boys and girls in Arusha on the topic "Grooming Self for Marriage." Prompted by the Spirit, my wife had a heavy burden to organize this seminar, with the help and participation of the above-mentioned executive committee members and other Christians who were willing to join hands with us. Three hundred youths, exactly the sitting capacity of the sanctuary of the Arusha Community Church that we had hired for the occasion, honored the invitation. My wife and I covered all the related organizational expenses! It rained that day, not in the neighborhood where we were, but only on the roof and compound of the Arusha Community Church where the seminar was taking place. This was how the youth ministry began in Arusha.

Today, the ministry is headed by a youth bureau elected by the general assembly during the last seminar held on 31 March 2012. It is composed of five young men and women as follows: a president (Joshua), a vice president, (Lilian), a secretary (Glory), a deputy secretary (Stephen), and a prayer coordinator (Thomas), essentially students and a teacher. The election of the bureau ran simply and smoothly, just as the Lord had predicted.

The youth bureau came as a welcome support to the executive committee which organizes also the seminars intended for the youths. The objective of the ministry is to bring youth to the knowledge of Christ, enable them grow in faith and in their daily walk with God, as well as prepare them for their family, professional, and social lives. My wife and I meet regularly in our home with the bureau members to share the Word, pray, praise the Lord, and train them in leadership.

To date, three major youth seminars have been organized to teach them life skills and instill in them the fear of God, in order to make them examples within their families, communities and even countries. Large numbers of young men and women usually attend.

Life as a Couple

Ours is very simple. As is the case with all human beings, our experience as a couple is characterized by ups and downs, apart from the great difference that we have built our union on the Rock, Our Lord Jesus Christ. In him and thanks to him, we share a life of mutual love and trust, and we live in peace and joy. We do the best we can to continue instructing our children in the way they should go (Proverbs 22:6), raising and guiding them by example. More than once, and in different circumstances, God has showed us how much he loves us. We are deeply grateful for His special love. It is this love that moves us and this love that keeps our hearts and home open to brothers and sisters in Christ, to our friends, colleagues, and neighbors in addition to members of our family to share the Word of God, our roof and our table, as well as build and edify ourselves mutually. We are still praying the Lord to teach us to do the same towards people we are not very familiar with and who are not in our immediate neighborhood.

That is my life.

It was in this context that, after having been unable to spend the end-of-year festive season with all our four daughters since the year 2000, my wife and I decided that we would all travel to Israel and spend Christmas in the Holy Land together.

TRIP TO THE HOLY LAND

It was with a lot of enthusiasm, hope, and faith that we had prepared this trip. We were looking forward to going to concretely witness the Word of God and walk in the footsteps of Jesus Christ. The period we had chosen for our trip ran from 22 to 30 December 2010. My wife, our third daughter, and I had to leave from Arusha, Tanzania, where we lived, and the three other girls from Ireland or the United States, where they were studying or working.

About ten days prior to our departure, we celebrated Christmas with our United Nations colleagues and their family members, shortly before their respective departures for the end-of-year holidays. This carols evening was organized by UN ICTR Christian Fellowship, on 7 December 2010. At our church, Dominion Restoration Church, we had celebrated our third anniversary and even organized the launching ceremony of the first CD of our choir on 15 December 2010. We were to leave Arusha for Nairobi on 18 December to catch our flight to Tel Aviv on 20 December.

A few days before we left, Eunice, our eldest daughter, who was working in Ireland, called us on Skype. She had something to tell us. This is what she said: "Daddy, Mummy, I was fasting because I really wanted to devote a few days to the Lord in prayer. I had a burden about my scholarship to enable me return to do my MBA in the United States. At the end of my fast, while I was praying, the Lord revealed to me something concerning our family—that is, concerning Daddy, Mummy, Diyenat, Maud, and Capucine."

Here, I will limit myself basically to what she told me about myself. "The Lord told me, 'I will make your father a new man.' When He said this, I immediately had a vision in which Daddy was speaking to a great crowd, as in a crusade, and as he laid his hands on people, they were healed…I found that quite strange. I couldn't tell what was going on."

I do recall that neither my wife nor I could make any sense out of this revelation. In fact, I still remember my wife cracking a small joke about it after our conversation with our daughter by saying, "The Lord will make you a new man. Does that mean you are not yet saved?" The jocular tone in which she said it really caused us to laugh very much. We continued carrying out our usual responsibilities and simply forgot about it all.

My wife, our daughter Diyenat, and I left Arusha for Nairobi on 18 December 2010 on an Impala bus. We spent two nights at the home of our friends, David and Jayne Mutiga, and their two children, Sheila and Brian, both young adults who had hosted us. May God bless this family abundantly for its generosity and commitment to advance the kingdom of God on earth!

On our way to the airport, we had to meet our pastor, Charles Akwera, and our beloved sister Edith and her husband, Kenneth, who were also in Nairobi for the weekend to visit the premises of a newly planted branch of our church. Unfortunately, on account of a huge traffic jam in the city, this was not possible. We were held back by traffic, and we decided to meet at the airport. We arrived there just on time to pray together and say good-bye. The pastor prayed and pleaded with God to bless us with his favor and protection.

When we arrived in Tel Aviv on 21 December 2010, representatives of the Israeli tour agency that had organized our guided trip to the Holy Land were there to welcome us. The said agency is called Vered Hasharon Tour, and it is owned by Danny Amir. We were taken to Metropolitan Hotel, where our rooms had been booked, and waited for the arrival of the three others who joined us on three different flights. On 22 December, there at our hotel, we met two employees of the travel agency, including Charity, a Kenyan who was their representative in Nairobi and with whom my wife communicated abundantly for the arrangements of our visit, and had dinner together in the restaurant of the hotel.

When we got back to our rooms, I gathered the family for a moment of prayer to thank the Lord for having brought us to the Holy Land and to prepare us to make the most of this trip. After we prayed, our daughter Maud indicated that the Lord had revealed something to her. He had told her, "You will remember this trip!"

Early morning on 22 December, driving a beautiful shuttle bus, our driver came to fetch us to begin our visit. His name was Isaac. He followed the route generally offered to Christians that our tour agency had suggested as follows:

- Canaan, which reminds us about the place where Jesus changed water into wine at the wedding, and there we bought two bottles of this famous wine as a souvenir.
- The Mount of Olives, where the Lord delivered the sermon on the beatitudes to the great crowd that had gathered there. The premises had been adapted into a place where individuals or families could meet to pray. Of course, I took advantage of this opportunity to call for a short prayer session for the family away from the other tourists. On that day, and according to my wife, I said a prayer that was going to be of great significance on the events that were to follow. Watching the videos of the trip, basically, I just thanked the Lord for the privilege of setting foot on the Holy Land, walking in the footsteps of our Lord Jesus Christ, and asked him to make sure that we do not leave that land the way we came.
- Capernaüm, the town of Jesus. We visited the remains of the house of Mary, the mother of Jesus.
- The Sea of Galilee on which we did a boat cruise, just to experience what the Lord used to do with his disciples.

- The point on the sea where Simon Peter and his friends were fishing but never made any catch until the Lord Jesus appeared and told them to cast their nets on the right side of the boat, from where they made a catch so great their nets could not contain it;

At the end of day 1, we were so emotional. We were so touched by what we saw at the various sites. Documented history just came alive as we went from one place to the other, and by the time we got back, we were awestruck.

In Tiberias, we spent the night of twenty-second breaking twenty-third of December before continuing towards Jerusalem. Here, my wife had a strange dream in which she heard a voice saying: "Leontine you have not yet started preparing your songs of praise. You have only one day and a half left."

During breakfast the next day, unable to understand what the Lord was saying, my wife narrated her dream to the children and me. We all felt this had to do with Christmas carols, given that the next day, 24 December, was going to be Christmas Eve. So we asked my wife to prepare a brief family devotion for Christmas with some carols, as she was wont to do. She could not get the rationale behind all this, especially as she was sure she had already done that during the Christmas Eve ceremony with UNICTR Christian Fellowship at our workplace. She agreed, nevertheless, to do so.

That morning, we went visiting Christian sites until 3:00 p.m., when we got to the River Jordan. There we found many people getting themselves baptized. Since my entire family and myself had already been baptized by immersion, we nevertheless decided to take a dive in the Jordan to rededicate our lives to the Lord. We were given white robes to go into the water. Two of our daughters, Diyenat and Capucine, my wife, and I got changed, while Eunice and Maud were busy snapping pictures and filming this moment for posterity.

I was the first to step into the water and took a good dive. Then I called my wife Leontine and immersed her in the river. Capucine followed suit. As I came out of the water to fetch Diyenat, who was waiting for her turn on the steps around the pool, to the amazement of my wife and children, I simply slumped on the stairs as if I had slipped, with both hands holding unto the bars of the ramp erected to guide tourists into and out of the water safely. My wife rushed to my rescue, followed by the children, and they all tried to bring me back to my feet. What exactly happened thereafter is nothing but a blurred picture in my mind. According to them, suddenly I was gone! They tried to do some reanimation.

An ambulance arrived and rushed me to a hospital in Tiberias, Poriya Medical Center, where a doctor revealed that I had had a brain hemorrhage. Since the hospital in Tiberias was not equipped to handle cases of this kind, around 8:00 pm, I was evacuated to Haifa, about two hours' drive from Tiberias, where you have Rambam Medical Center, the biggest hospital in Israel.

There, on that 24 December 2010, from 8:00 am to 1:00 pm, according to the neurosurgeons, I underwent two operations, one immediately after the other. The first set out to clean my brain that was flooded by blood, following the rupture of an aneurysm, while the second was meant to stitch the cervical vein that had ruptured. I was supposed to come out of both operations only on 26 December 2010, going by the fact that the neurosurgeon who operated me last had intimated to my wife that I was going to be unconscious for two days consecutively. My brain had been so tampered with that he had given me medication to keep me down, asleep, for that period of time. But then to their great surprise, I was not coming around at all. I sank into a coma.

If I wrote this book, it is because of what I saw during this coma. And my prayer is that you will be touched and transformed as I was by this experience.

DURING THE COMA

What struck me the most during the coma was the landscape. I was fully surrounded by an unending stretch of land just like a desert, no tree at all. The scenery was basking in the soft glow of a yellowish gold light. And yet in all this, not a shadow was found. Everything was lit with the same intensity, as if the light went across every object it met.

My spirit hovered from one place to the other, and its movement was instantaneous. I could cover long distances at the speed light. I went from one location to another. The landscape was clear, while the earth and the sky merged beautifully at the edge of the limitless horizon. It was impossible to distinguish the beginning from the end. Permit me to use the surface of the sea and the sky as an illustration—as you sail on the sea, it would appear the sky runs into the sea out there in the horizon. That was the impression I had. The sky and the sea seemed to have the same meeting point.

At a certain moment, I came to a standstill at a wide space; it looked like a big football stadium. I found myself at the centre of the stadium. All around me were the shadows of many people seated in the terraces, many people whose faces I could not see. They were clothed with white and light blue linens. I was at the centre of the arena, and I felt like all the spectators had their eyes glued on me. All of a sudden came a loud voice that said with authority:

"You are all like children, who after playing outside, burst into the living room where their father is resting."

"Flee from sin!"

"Avoid vain wrangling!"

After hearing these words, I was immediately transported to another location, where I discovered a congregation praising God in songs and prayer, and suddenly whisked off into another location, before a huge basin full of a liquid looking like water. This liquid moved back and forth like waves in the sea, without spilling over.

The same voice said to me, "This liquid before you represents all the prayers and the praise from below. That is where they are all preserved."

The basin itself is an illustration to remind us about the existence of God who controls our lives.

As if to provide an explanation, the following image is brought to my mind. As a parent, you have your child all dressed up in white to attend a party. While you are getting yourself ready, the child is distracted and begins to play. And then you find him in his dress spotted with stains. Try to imagine your reaction as a parent. You lose your temper, and you just get mad. You need to take time to change the child once more. Do you not run the risk of missing the party by so doing? Will this situation not simply spoil the party?

That is what it is for me, your heavenly Father. I have already dressed you in white for the banquet. Do not soil yourselves!

A Bible verse is brought to my mind:

> Do you not know that your body is a temple of the Holy Spirit who is in you, whom you have from God, and that you are not your own? For you have been bought with a price: therefore glorify God in your body.
>
> 1 Corinthians 6:19–20 (NASB)

Then, another verse, Titus 3:9, "But avoid foolish controversies and genealogies and strife and disputes about the Law, for they are unprofitable and worthless."

OUT OF COMA

When I woke up, I was surprised to hear that I had been gone—that I had been lifeless on a hospital bed in Israel for twelve days in an intensive care unit, breathing and being kept "alive" through machines—and that I was about to be evacuated to France for further treatment and physiotherapy to learn how to speak, to walk, and to remember things again. I had no pain anywhere. My wife describes this experience in her book entitled *From the Jordan River to His Bedside*.

The three aforementioned messages delivered by the voice left me deeply touched and broken. I am convinced that he first has to do with the whole concept of instilling the fear of the Lord. The second invites us to holiness as recommended by God. The third exhorts us to have good relationships among ourselves as brethren and to live in unity, be it within the church, the family, the society.

Since that day, I have only one desire: share this message with as many people as possible. I felt that putting it in writing may be the ideal way of doing so. The voice that I heard is still loud and clear in my mind.

Do Not Tease God in His Sanctuary!

What does *to tease* mean? According to the dictionary, this word means "to make noise, to create disorder, to exasperate."

As for the word *tease*, it means to "cause a row, a fuss, or a scene." According to the dictionary of the French Academy (eighth edition), it refers to a disorderly dance and, by extension, to a disorderly dance and tumult caused by pupils. For the *Littré* dictionary, this has to do with a dance that was so indecent it was prohibited in public places by the police.

It is worthwhile to note that for God to make us the temple of the Holy Spirit, it is an honor and a privilege. This is a calling that demands gravity and integrity. Do you remember the Bible passage in which "Jesus drove traders out of the temple?" We must not transform our bodies into market places.

> On reaching Jerusalem, Jesus entered the temple courts and began driving out those who were buying and selling there. He overturned the tables of the moneychangers and the benches of those selling doves, and would not allow anyone to carry merchandise through the temple courts. And as he taught them, he said, "Is it not written: 'My house will be called a house of prayer for all nations'? But you have made it 'a den of robbers.'" Mark 11: 15–17 (NIV)

Why Must We Flee from Sin?

In the Bible, Roman 6:23 states, "For the wages of sin is death, but the gift of God is eternal life through Christ Jesus our Lord" (KJV).

In order to resist and avoid useless internal struggles, it is better to avoid being tempted at all to remain sober, praising the Lord all the time. We are all aware that the wages of sin is death and that in John 10: 10, Jesus tells us, "The thief comes only to steal, to kill and to destroy; I came that they may have life, and have it abundantly (NASB).

Satan came to steal, to kill, and to destroy. His aim was—and remains—to steal, to kill, and to destroy particularly all men and, above all, to steal, to kill, and to destroy the church of the Lord. He uses many tactics to turn us away from God. Jesus Christ told the Pharisees in John 8:44:

> You are of your father the devil, and your will is to do your father's desires. He was a murderer from the beginning, and does not stand in the truth, because there is no truth in him. When he lies, he speaks out of his own character, for he is a liar and the father of lies.
>
> John 8:44 (ESV)

By seducing us and leading us astray, the devil is out to estrange us from God. Once he does this, we become vulnerable before him and he can manipulate us at will. He tells us lies to achieve his goals, for he is the father of lies. He is like a fisherman with a line that has a hook hidden in an earthworm and is thrown into the sea to attract fish. The fish that see just the earthworm wiggling at the end of the hook rush happily and blindly to swallow, oblivious of the danger it is facing. The consequence is that the next minute, that fish will find itself out of the water, far from its natural habitat, because it has been caught and inevitably ends up in the stomach of the fisherman.

We Christians are exactly like fish in water. We allow ourselves to be attracted by bait in our daily lives, seduced by the devil who uses material things, such as worldly property and pleasures to arouse our desires so as to eventually destroy us. Permit me to cite a few examples below.

Dancing

To the best of my knowledge, not once in the Bible are we told that dancing is a sin. Dancing is a way in which man expresses humility before God. For instance, David danced before the ark of God. By his behavior, David humbled himself before the Lord, His God. In the Psalms, we are exhorted to praise the Lord with dancing and musical instruments. It is therefore proper that we all as children of God should dance for our God during praise and worship.

> Praise the Lord! Praise God in his sanctuary; praise him in his mighty heavens!
> Praise him for his mighty deeds; praise him according to his excellent greatness!
> Praise him with trumpet sound; praise him with lute and harp!
> Praise him with tambourine and dance; praise him with strings and pipe!
> Praise him with sounding cymbals; praise him with loud clashing cymbals!
> Let everything that has breath praise the Lord! Praise the Lord!
>
> Psalm 150:1–6 (ESV)

However, dancing becomes a sin when it is about us. This is when the body dances for its own pleasure, simply to satisfy its carnal desires. This is when you dance for yourself or someone else, and there are body movements and gestures that arouse the flesh and whip up sexual desire. That is the example of a man and woman who may dance outside wedlock to express their illicit love, which eventually ends up in immorality (1 Corinthians 6:13).

Dancing becomes a sin once it is done to honor a man. In the Bible, John the Baptist lost his head simply because Herod's daughter danced well before him and his guests at his birthday party. Very pleased with her dancing performance, Herod told her she could ask for anything from him. The girl sought advice from her mother, who told her to ask for the head of John the Baptist on a platter. She got it. You should recall that Herod's wife had a grudge against John the Baptist, who unrelentingly and publicly denounced their adulterous relationship. That was the ideal opportunity Herod's wife had been waiting for—to do away with this man of God who was a nuisance to their lust-ridden lives (Matthew 14: 6–11).

We must dance for God alone and not for men.

How can dancing insidiously affect a blessing?

By way of example, imagine a religious wedding ceremony that closes with a gala dance in worldly music. All things being equal, we should close our wedding celebration in praise and worship just to glorify God and thank him. The Bible urges us to praise the Lord with dancing and musical instruments. It is therefore obvious that this has nothing to do with dancing for ourselves, or dancing to please men, but rather an occasion to humble one's self before God and express gratitude for this marital union, for this new covenant and for the happiness, joy and blessing which comes with marriage.

Marriage is a ceremony that takes place before God and men. God honors and blesses the marital union. How, therefore, can we give honor to God and to the devil at the same time? That is one of the ills plaguing marriages that are celebrated these days. While this may appear harmless, it may just be an open door the enemy may subsequently use at will. Within a couple, out of the blue, we are faced with misunderstandings, quarrels, barrenness or delayed pregnancies, coldness in prayer or even prayerlessness. The Lord is pushed very far away, and the couple finds itself in confusion, which leads to divorce to the joy of our enemy, the devil.

> Unless the Lord builds the house,
> They labor in vain who build it;
> Unless the Lord guards the city,
> The watchman stays awake in vain.
>
> Psalms 127: 1 (NKJV)

A wedding built on the Rock, Jesus Christ, is blessed by God. The Lord grants that home a heritage. "Behold, children are a heritage from the Lord; the fruit of the womb is a reward" (Psalms 127:3 ESV).

How Do We Tease God?

Here, let me mention a few examples drawn from everyday life.

1. In Our Studies

For us Christians, studies through the acquisition of diplomas and diverse certificates which open doors to well-paid jobs that put an end to the burden of poverty imposed by the devil, is one of the ways of getting honestly and freely to the promised land.

If we Christians work very hard without resorting to witch doctors, access to the different social positions will be made easy by our success. We will be able to walk over all educational barriers of the social system.

Working hard at your studies is a way of obeying and honoring God! In light of the resources at our disposal, let us honor him by excelling in our studies, failing at which, we dishonor him.

> Finally then, brethren, we request and exhort you in the Lord Jesus, that as you received from us instruction as to how you ought to walk and please God (just as you actually do walk), that you excel still more.
>
> 1 Thessalonians 4:1 (NASB)

2. At Our Workplaces

If we are blessed with a job, when there are millions of others who are hunting for jobs, we must do our work with professionalism and enthusiasm, as doing it for God and not just for ourselves or just to earn a living. "Whatever you do, work at it with all your heart, as working for the Lord, not for human masters" (Colossians 3:23 NIV).

According to Rick Warren, Apostle Paul exhorts us to work "as for the Lord and not for men." In other words, he is saying that there is no job that is too small, too low, or too insignificant for anyone who has the right motives and pursues them for good reason. If I do my work, not for the boss but for the Lord, excellence will be my goal. We should have the following attitude: "I am doing this for God. I will work as if it was for God."

How can I tell if I am working for God? My attitude will bear the following hallmarks: excellence and enthusiasm. Firstly, if I do my work not for my boss but for the Lord, I will aim for excellence. That means that I will do the utmost I can—I will work as hard as possible because the only approval that matters to me is approval from God. I will act excellently to the best of my ability. In addition, I will work with enthusiasm, as doing so for God. My attitude will always be joyful. "Never flag in zeal, and never be lazy" (Romans 12:11).

So we are bound to respect the labor contract laid down by our employers. In Congo-Brazzaville, my fatherland, we say, "It is eight hours of work and not eight hours at work." It is morally unacceptable to go to the office, sit down. and twiddle your thumbs or play cards on your computer to while time away, simply waiting for the end of the day to return home, having ticked off your day as done. Is that not treachery towards your employer and even towards God? Our attitude vis-à-vis the organization, its property or even colleagues at work, may leave much to be desired. This will open doors for criticisms from on lookers, especially unbelievers, who will revile our testimony as Christians and drag the name of the Lord in mud. Many are deceived to believe that in the crowd, their evil deeds go unnoticed or unknown. In Psalm 11: 4 it is written: "The Lord is in his holy temple; the Lord's throne is in heaven; his eyes see, his eyelids test the children of man" (ESV).

Therefore, the Lord sees all men and women and analyzes their deeds. And contrary to what those who challenge God's existence say, the Lord is not indifferent to whatever happens on earth—all things are "transparent" before God and he will bring all to judgment through his son, the Lord Jesus Christ. This truth is further buttressed in Proverbs 15:3: "The eyes of the Lord are in every place, keeping watch on the evil and the good" (ESV).

We easily forget that men, who are mere creatures, can only see that which is visible, that which has shape, while God sees the heart. God is omniscient, and with just a glance, he sees the visible and the invisible.

Such bad employees will face difficulties in their careers. Either they will not know any promotion or growth within the company or they will lose their jobs abruptly and find easy scapegoats ("My boss does not like me," "My relatives have bewitched me," "My colleagues are jealous and want to destroy me," etc.). They look everywhere else to find reason for their professional malaise.

If we as Christians sign any contracts before God, we ought to respect such, honor them. When we work with all our hearts, motivated by the love of Christ, our work will be an act of worship towards God. What is the attitude you display at your workplace?

3. Within the Couple and the Family

Many Christian couples behave like blind people. The fact that you are Christians does not exclude vigilance and alertness. In 1 Peter 5:8, the Bible says: "Be sober, be vigilant; because your adversary the devil walks about like a roaring lion, seeking whom he may devour" (NKJV).

Resist him with the power of faith and a life of prayer. To avoid any dead ends, you must entrust all into the hands of the Lord—that is, surrender your life, your family, and your property into his hands. You should do this more so because the couple and the marital home make up the first church of Christ. They represent the house of God. God must be at the centre of everything, the focal point in all activities therein. The couple therefore trusts God in all it undertakes, without doubting that he will intervene.

In the home, God's principles which are laid down in the Ten Commandments as well as in the recommendations by Apostle Paul must be applied.

> "Wives, submit to your own husbands, as to the Lord. For the husband is the head of the wife even as Christ is the head of the church, his body, and is himself its Savior. Now as the church submits to Christ, so also wives should submit in everything to their husbands. Husbands, love your wives, as Christ loved the church and gave himself up for her, that he might sanctify her, having cleansed her by the washing of water with the word, so that he might present the church to himself in splendor, without spot or wrinkle or any such thing, that she might be holy and without blemish. In the same way husbands should love their wives as their own bodies. He who loves his wife loves himself. For no one ever hated his own flesh, but nourishes and cherishes it, just as Christ does the church.
>
> Ephesians 5: 22–29 (ESV)

Unfortunately, the selfishness of the human being, his desire to dominate, jealousy, covetousness, and the challenges of modern society fuel misunderstandings, strife, quarrels, the lust for power, and the love of money, which cause tension within the couple and the family such that they end up on the rocks.

4. *In Christian Communities*

Generally speaking, Christian communities tend unfortunately to be arenas for vain and useless debates and quarrels concerning the law and doctrines. This denomination is better than the other. That denomination does not believe in the work of the Holy Spirit nor in the healing power of our Lord Jesus Christ. That other denomination preaches only prosperity and does not lay enough emphasis on Jesus Christ and the salvation he brings. It is a real tug-of-war. It is an outright competition—in fact, a full-blown contest in terms of which denomination has the highest number of members, the highest number of prophecies, the greatest manifestation of the gift of healing. It is all such considerations that alienate Christians from what is essential: the great commission that Our Lord Jesus Christ stated in Mark 16:15: "And He said to them, 'Go into all the world and preach the gospel to all creation'" (NIV).

A community may organize an outreach campaign or celebrate Jesus within the "March for Jesus" initiative and invite other Christians to join in for a greater impact. Unfortunately, we find that leaders of certain communities or churches either refuse to show up or stop their parishioners from attending for reasons best known to them, and very often very selfish reasons. Or if and when they themselves do attend, they do so but dissuade their members from attending, lest they lose them. As a result, the impact of the evangelization is reduced.

Sometimes the conditions laid down for their participation are so stringent they discourage the community that is organizing the event. For them to attend preparatory meetings, drinks or food should be guaranteed, fuel should be provided for them to be able to travel, a car should be made available, or airtime should be bought for their telephones by which they will reach their friends or counterparts, money should be given as a contribution for their choir or intercessory groups to participate. There should be a guarantee that all offerings to be collected will be shared and things of that nature. All this may be so burdensome for the organizer that he gives up and ends up organizing the campaign alone.

We forget that all these communities that claim they are Christians should have Jesus Christ as their foundation and that Christ is one and the same for all and for His church.

As for our different churches, the situation is even worse. You have unnecessary quarrels between the senior pastor and his assistants, between the pastor and his elders and or deacons, on church administrative issues, the use of the tithes and offerings that come in, the absence or the presence of the five ministries named in Ephesians 4:11–15.

> And He Himself gave some to be apostles, some prophets, some evangelists, and some pastors and teachers, for the equipping of the saints for the work of ministry, for the edifying of the body of Christ, till we all come to the unity of the faith and of the knowledge of the Son of God, to a perfect man, to the measure of the stature of the fullness of Christ; that we should no longer be children, tossed to and fro and carried about with every wind of doctrine, by the trickery of men, in the cunning craftiness of deceitful plotting, but, speaking the truth in love, may grow up in all things into Him who is the head—Christ—
>
> Ephesians 4:11–15 (NKJV)

At the end of the day, the church is divided and even ruined, with the assistant pastors or elders leaving the church and taking along with them many of the parishioners to start their own churches. Members of the same church do not go unaffected, as the same cankerworm attacks the various departments, in particular, the choir, the women's group, intercession team, ushers, Sunday school, and the list goes on. They spend their time debating on venial issues or criticizing the pastor or his wife, the church officials, or other members on issues that have nothing to do with their ministry. We have heard criticisms on the dressing of this brother or that sister. We have witnessed stiff competition between members of the same department or even between entire groups as they seek to outmatch the other to be in the good books of the pastor or enjoy his favor, and yet our eyes should be on the Lord Jesus Christ and not on any man, regardless of his title.

All the various church departments, which are indeed holy places, operate under the power of God and are called to serve and glorify him and him alone. The choir, for example, is a key instrument to praise God in the church. By the way it is, it should be able to stand before the congregation and render ministry worthy of God's service.

The youth ministry is called to represent the future of the church. It should incarnate the hope for a bright tomorrow and must be decent, disciplined, and obedient to the Word of God. It must operate abiding by the principles of the Bible and applying it faithfully. As for the college of elders, and according to the criteria laid down within each local church, this could be the link pin or coordinating organ between the church and the Pastor. This team could ensure that there is discipline and good governance within the church. It could advise and counsel various church members and assist the Pastor in his mission as the shepherd of the flock.

Any distorted use of any of these groups comes across as disturbing or teasing God. And such behavior before God is sin.

From the day I came back to life, I recovered, resumed my work and my service in the kingdom of God, most of my Bible readings and meditations are more focused on the message I received from God. I wish to share hereunder what the Holy Spirit has instilled in me concerning the fear of God.

How to Fear God?

The Bible says, "The fear of the lord is the beginning of wisdom" (Proverbs 9:10 ESV).

We are called upon to fear God by the way we live—that is to say the way we speak, think and act. We are the temple of God and by virtue of that fact, we are the dwelling place of God. So long as it is indeed an honor to be the dwelling place of God, on that score, we cannot afford to soil it.

How Do We Defile the Temple of God?

Jesus reminded us that we should not engage our bodies in immorality, drunkenness, fornication, adultery, or prostitution. Our bodies are temples, and so if we defile these temples, we are defiling ourselves.

Can you imagine a garbage truck dumping all it has collected from the neighborhood in the living room of our house? If that happened, then the Holy Spirit will be aggrieved and forced to quit until the temple is again tidied up. In the meantime, we will face the consequences of his absence, as is the case with people living without God. Life without God is a terrible nightmare. Life without God is like living without your immunity or defense mechanism, as is the case of a person contaminated by AIDS. As a result, we are exposed to any bacterial or viral attack, which may lead to spiritual and even physical death.

Praise and prayer are two weapons that can secure divine protection for us, and with these weapons, we have the power to resist and push back all the enemy's attacks. If only we have the fear of God, we will find the needed wisdom to trample over the enemy. The Lord inhabits the praises of his children, and when we praise God, he abides in that atmosphere of praise and the enemy flees far away from us. No sickness can resist the power of God when his glory rests upon us.

We must offer ourselves to God as a living sacrifice smitten by the fire, of a sweet smelling fragrance rising towards God. Integrity is another character trait that will draw us closer to God and make us resemble our heavenly Father.

We Fear God by Avoiding Vain Wrangling

In the home, spouses should mutually avoid tempting one another to commit this sin. This simply implies that spouses should know their respective limits, how far they can go. It is not because the husband or the wife can bear some things that the partner should continue to provoke him or her.

Since lack of forgiveness is unacceptable before God (Colossians 3:13), forgiveness should be the golden rule governing each couple. It is like taking a refreshing bath every morning and every evening.

Through prayer, we talk to God our heavenly Father, and that draws us closer to Him. If God is for us, who can be against us?" (Romans

8:31). If God lives in a couple, who can do anything against that couple? No evil force can destabilize it. Such a couple will be like a tree planted by a stream and which will be watered so much it will never face any drought; each season it will bear its fruit (Psalm 1). Here, the stream is Christ, Our Savior.

In the community, members should be motivated to love one another out of love for Christ. Here, there should be no room for jealousy or envy since the love of Christ does not wrong anyone, forgives and forgets. Members of the community should love one another, help one another, and stand with one another in the name of Jesus Christ. Divisions and gossip should be banished from the community. Mutual respect should be restored, and crowned with the fear of the Lord.

God expects us to display respect towards each other during worship and church activities and expects that decisions should be arrived at by consensus, while allowing the Holy Spirit to move freely. How can we claim to love God whom we do not see when we hate our own very brothers, whom we see?

As temples of the Holy Spirit, we should keep ourselves clean, both inside and outside. Our duty is to please God, as a wise child would please his parents. We must not live like persons crossing the corridor of temptation. This is a parable about two men who had set out on a journey. All through the journey, one of them was happy to walk straight on, moving in front of the other and without any concern about whatever was happening around him. Much to the contrary, the second was caught up with things along the way, and he just grabbed all that pleased him to the extent that he became quite heavy. Along the way, both men got to a river they had to swim across. The first swam without any difficulty, right across to the other bank. As for the second, with all he was carrying, he could not swim. He sank and got drowned.

The first had a warm welcome on the other side of the river, where he found a great fortune. The second lost his life as a result of covetousness and the love of worldly pleasures. We can draw a big lesson from this parable and recall what Jesus said in Matthew 6:33–34: "But seek ye first the kingdom of God, and his righteousness; and all these things shall be added unto you" (KJV).

Life is indeed like a walk through the corridor of temptation, where we are tempted by silver and gold, attracted by power and the attractiveness of this world, just as Jesus was tempted in the desert by the devil who offered him the glory of the world if only He would bow down and worship him (Matthew 4:1–11). Let us not be deceived by the devil who is brandishing the material riches of this world to seduce us.

MEDICAL EVACUATION

I came out of coma but could not remember anything. My memory had received a shock, especially my immediate memory. Physically, my skin had dried up and my body had looked like it was covered with white scales. My old skin that was like a white covering from my neck to the soles of my feet was falling off in shreds. I thank God for giving me a new skin. My neurosurgeon assured my wife that this was going to pass. He also indicated to her that I was now in a position to fly back home to continue the treatment if she so wished. This is how my family, in consultation with my employer, the International Criminal Tribunal for Rwanda, decided to send me back to France, to Bretonneau Hospital in Tours, to complete my treatment and undergo physiotherapy and relearn how to speak, to think, to revamp my memory, and to walk.

That was when one of the biggest Israeli aircrafts of Air Halal company was chartered for my health evacuation from Tel Aviv to Paris. The entire first-class compartment was reserved for me and the neurosurgeon who was to accompany me to Paris. The aircraft flew straight back to Tel Aviv after one hour on the tarmac at the Charles de Gaulle airport in Paris.

There again, we saw God's hand at work in the interest of his children—at the right time and at the right place.

CONCLUSION

From time immemorial, in one way or other, God has always spoken to men through dreams, visions, revelations, or prophecies (Acts 2:17–18). The experience I just shared with you is consistent with God's faithfulness towards us and faithfully tallies with his Word, the Bible. If I was touched in this manner, then God may have deemed it right to make me his humble mouthpiece at this point in time.

In light of the foregoing account therefore, let us urge one another to remain faithful servants and worshippers of the Living God, for we owe our lives to him and he deserves our praise, worship, and gratitude.

God is right here! He is real and present in our lives through his Son Jesus Christ, who gave his life on the cross of Calvary for us and continues to love us so that we can become presentable and pleasing before God.

What should our motto be? Our motto should be loyalty and committed service to God!

To you, men and servants of God, church leaders, may I humbly say that it is imperative the teachings be focused more on holiness and the fear of God, on the urgent need to keep the body, which is the temple of God, clean, and on the importance of working in unity and securing the approval of the leaders and the brethren in matters of decision-making, to ensure growth and smooth running of the church? And that it is crucial to strive to be living models who practice what they teach?

To fathers and mothers in Christian families, it is important to institute family devotion during which you study the Bible in your homes, pray and have fellowship with the children in order to inculcate in them the fear of God and the importance of living according to his Word. It is unavoidable that before your children you become the example to follow when it comes to the principles of life you wish to impart to them and have nothing to do with those who say, "Do what I say and not what I do." By so doing, the home will become the first church of Christ.

To you the youth, please note that regardless of your age, God can use you as his messenger anytime and anywhere. God used Eunice and Maud Mabika, our daughters, to warn my wife and other children about what was going to happen in my life. In the kingdom of God, and according to the will of God, you can be either a vessel of wood or clay for ignoble use or a vessel of gold or silver for noble purposes (2 Timothy 2:19–22). What matters is that you show that you are available to be used by God the way he deems fit. On this score, age is of little or no importance. What you need to know is that above all else, you are created by God and created by God for a specific purpose. For that reason, you must bear in mind the fact that the way you live as you grow into adulthood must be in a manner that speaks of devotion to God, so that before Him you are pure and beyond reproach. You must avoid immorality and other sins connected to worldly pleasures that soil your body, which is the temple of God.

To you who have read this testimony, but do not yet know the Lord, I urgently pray that you seek to know him so as to give a meaning to your life. God is not far away. All it takes is a short prayer and you will be in touch with Him. Sincerely and wholeheartedly repeat the following:

> Almighty God, though I do not yet know you, I would like to know you. I confess that I have sinned against You in thoughts, in words and in deeds. Forgive me. Come into my heart. Take control of my life and guide me as from this day. All this I pray in the name of Your Son Jesus Christ, Amen!

By this simple prayer, you have started out on an extraordinary journey with the Lord Jesus Christ. At the end of this journey, and if you hold fast and go all the way, you will hear him say, "Well done, good and faithful servant. You have been faithful over a little; I will set you over much. Enter into the joy of your master" (Matthew 25:21 ESV).

To you who have read this testimony, and who are privileged to have known the Lord, I pray that you will be so edified about the reality of Our Savior Jesus Christ, that you will immediately sit up and adjust your life such that it will honor him and at the appointed time, he will welcome you with the words of Matthew 25:21, quoted heretofore.

To close, I wish to thank you Lord once again for the extraordinary experience I went through! Thank you from the depths of my heart for enabling me to write this testimony and its accompanying message in order to share it with as many as possible to edify your body, the Church, and glorify your name!

To you be all the honor and glory, now and forever. Amen!

Your beloved,
—Pascal

The family today by Charles Obe

Leontine and Pascal Mabika, Coordinators of Family Life and Youth Ministries, singers and authors

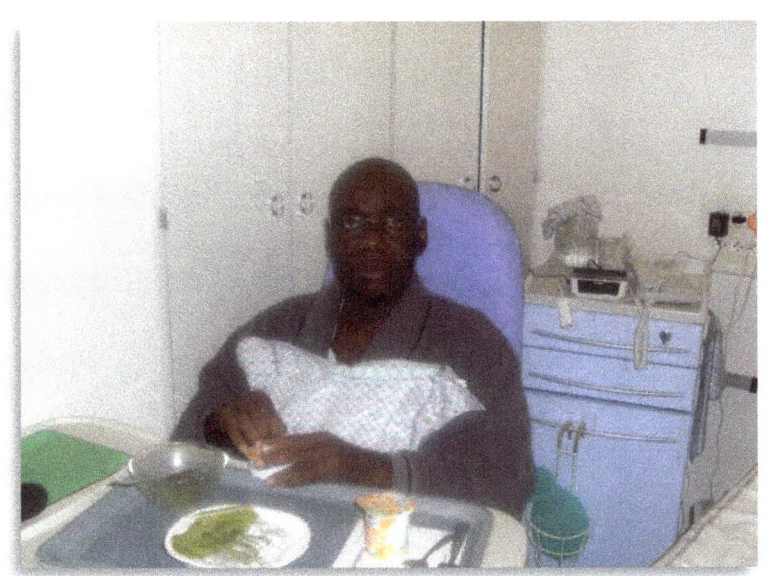

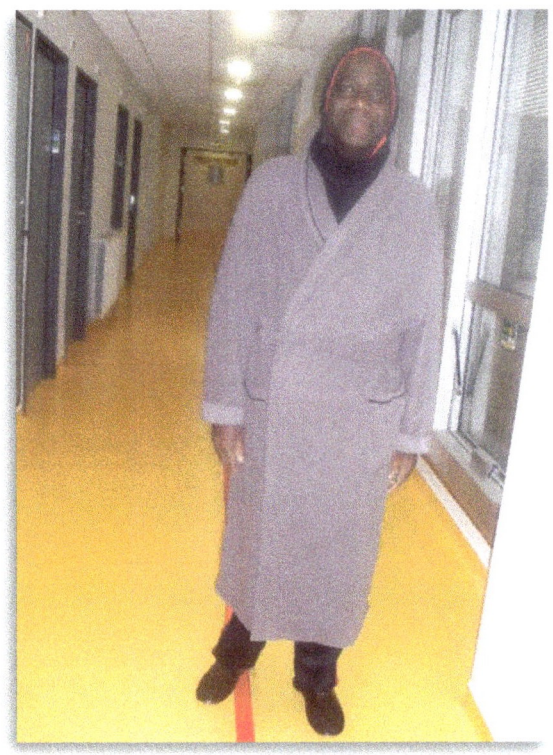

Pascal in the hospital

Our four daughters on the boat sail in the Sea of Galilee

Pascal and I praying during a site visit

The family in Capharnaum

The Family next to the Sea of Galilee

Pascal Mabika alone in the hall of the Metropolitant Hotel in Tel Aviv upon arrival in Israel

the shadow of death, I will fear no evil: for thou art with me; thy rod and thy staff they comfort me" (Ps 23:4).

To you who have taken time to read this book, please understand all this did not happen by chance. It is for a purpose. The Bible says in Psalms 37:23, "The steps of a good man are ordered by the Lord: and he delighteth in his way." This means that what the Lord, in his love and grace, has done for us, he is faithful and just enough to do it also for you. Just make sure your relationship with him is where it ought to be.

If you know the Lord Jesus as your personal Savior, I encourage you to maintain the course and develop your intimacy with him, which is God's priority for our lives. If you have backslidden, I urge you to come back to your first love and reinvite God into your life. If you have not yet accepted Jesus as your personal God and Savior, I beg you to do so in order to give meaning to your life. It is so simple. Just repeat this prayer after me: "Lord, I thank you for this opportunity. I invite you in my heart. Take control of my life and lead me. In Jesus's name, I pray. Amen!"

You have just embarked on a fantastic *journey* with the Son of God. Your life will never be the same again. And the Lord will surely show it to you! Congratulations and welcome to the assembly of the saints!

Heavenly Father, I thank you for giving me this platform to share your wonderful and mighty acts. As you said in 2 Timothy 1:8, "Be not thou therefore ashamed of the testimony of our Lord," I have written this book in obedience to you, Lord, the giver of the gift, and to the glory of your name!

With Love,
Your Daughter Leontine Birangui Mabika

afterward, when things turned out to be so different from what we had thought. However, in those trying times, our heavenly Father was ever present—he gave us power and faith to fast and pray, he answered our prayers by leading us into what to do. I am so thankful I obeyed the Spirit when he talked to me and my daughters supported me. In obedience, we acted for days in ways which seemed foolish in the eyes of men: reading scriptures, singing songs of praise, praying to Pascal's ear while he was in coma, and me touching his lifeless body with my hands as I was directed to. We did these things in turns, one after the other, to the amazement of the nurses and the relatives of the other patients in the ICU.

The Lord also provided for all our needs. When we left Israel, I did not have to pay a penny to the hospital. All was paid for by our medical-insurance company. I did not have to pay for the hotel bills that had piled up. Danny, the manager of Vered H. Tour took care of all the bills, and I was to refund him only later on. I did not pay a single penny for the medical evacuation to France, neither for my ticket nor for those of my husband and the accompanying neurosurgeon. Our employer did. My husband traveled like a king—on board a powerful Israeli aircraft, 777 type, in an entire *first class* compartment totally rearranged for that purpose and dedicated to him and the doctor alone. Above all, my husband is totally healed—he drives, works, and cares for his family. Most importantly, he shares his testimony whenever and wherever possible.

It can *only* be God! And we the Mabika family are so so grateful to our amazing and loving God!

God has given me songs, both lyrics and music, which my husband and I have recorded, and the CD is entitled *Lamb of God*, and this to the glory of his name.

I am convinced that the trials we all go through in life are stepping stones that God uses to move us to higher grounds. It might not be simple for you to see that while you are in the trial, but Almighty God is there in the trial with you! "Yea, though I walk through the valley of

CONCLUSION

As the Mabika family, we ask ourselves several questions, including this particular one: why did Pascal's aneurysm—which could have, all these years, erupted anywhere, be it in Arusha, in France, or in the United States, and anytime during the many trips he has undertaken—chose to burst only in the Holy Land, all the more so immediately after a dip in the Jordan River and while the whole family was gathered in one place, the last Christmas spent together dating back to ten years from the incident?

God said in the book of Jeremiah that he knows the plans that he has for us, plans to prosper us and not to harm us, plans to give us a hope and a future. We believe that there must be a purpose for that Israel experience in our lives. God has something in mind, and our prayer is that that purpose be fulfilled in Jesus's name!

Indeed, our family has been transformed as a result of this unique experience in Israel. Our personal walk with God has taken a new dimension as well as our family covenant with him. My husband is today indeed "a new man," as the Lord had said. Those things that used to bother him big time in the past do not matter anymore. He is convinced that the years God has added to his life have a specific purpose—for him to share the message that God gave him while in coma. You may want to refer to his book entitled *Twelve Days in Coma* for the details.

God spoke to the family, through Eunice and Maud, of what was to come. The ways of the Lord being well above our ways and his thoughts well above our thoughts (Isa 55:8), we did not really understand until

My heartfelt appreciation and gratitude to our family members and my sisters and their families; our spiritual parents, Charles and Judith Akwera of Dominion Restoration Church in Arusha; the women and men of God; friends of our daughters, brothers, and sisters in Christ all over the world, whom God used to love us and support us during that trying time; Zion City Church, Bethel Word Outreach Church Sokoine 1, Nairobi Pentecostal Church Valley Road, the Evangelical Church of Congo, the United Nations community; the churches in Dublin, in the United States of America, and in Israel; the neurosurgeons, medics, and other medical personnel of Poriya Medical Center in Tiberias and Rambam Hospital in Haifa—to you all, may God bless you, your homes, your ministries, and your businesses!

To you who were God' s vessels to support us spiritually through prayer and fasting, through a word of encouragement or word of wisdom, through sharing of the Word, may God richly reward you!

To you who labored for us behind the scenes, who we did not see or even know, may God who sees in the secret increase you and touch you at the point of your need!

My special thanks and blessings to Zoe, whom God put on my way, for her loving heart and sacrificial gift to this project by typing this manuscript despite her own workload. May God pour out his blessings upon you and your family headed by my longtime friend and UN colleague, George Frank!

must remember that God promised us that we will be victorious. In John 16:33, Jesus says "I have told you these things, so that in me you may have peace. In this world, you will have trouble. But take heart! I have overcome the world."

So whatever circumstances you are enduring, keep faith, focus on God, pray and believe in His word because we do not get "stuck" in a bad situation, but we go "through" a bad situation! Meaning there will be an end to all your troubles. So Trust in God for He is the only one who will see you through.

Vote of Thanks

My family and I would like, first of all, to express our wholehearted thanks to the Lord for the great miracle he served to us, to the glory of his mighty name! His name as Jehovah Rapha, the Lord who heals and the Lord who raises the dead materialized in our lives! Father, you are amazing! We will always talk about that wonderful act that you accomplished in the lives of our family. You spoke to your daughters about what was to come. You predicted it. You brought it to pass. You saw us through. May you be forever exalted!

I would like to give thanks to the Lord for our four daughters. They are indeed a heritage from the Lord. Without their faith and trust in God, their love for their dad, their confidence in me, and, mostly, their obedience, things would not have turned the way they did. The Lord rewarded their heart and our unity in prayer! May God use them as His instruments to change their generation!

describe the despair I felt at the moment. However, somehow, Isaiah 43:18–19 came through my mind and reassured me that the Lord was at work, and indeed He was.

The one thing I would say about this whole experience is that the Lord moves through our faith, our praise and worship, and through our unity. These are the 3 main components that made us strong and hopeful.

Let the Lord be Glorified for His is Faithful!"

Capucine

The experience that I endured in Israel is one of the most memorable experiences in my life. I truly learned the meaning of prayer and perseverance. Seeing how God answered our numerous prayers showed me how Faithful our God is. Prayer is so crucial in the life of a Christian.

There was no room for doubt, for as long as we prayed, we knew and strongly believed that God will do a miracle and use this situation for His Glory.

I could see that physically and emotionally my mother was tired, but spiritually she was stronger than ever! She would wake up early, pray and worship Him and I could honestly say that Prayer gave us all strengths to endure this difficult time. I have learned through the actions of my mother what it truly means to be a faithful woman of God and a faithful wife.

What to draw from this experience?

What you can draw from this experience is that in this life, we will go through hard times, difficult times, time of pain, sadness, confusion, tribulation, but we is broad that leads to destruction but the road is narrow that leads to life. Are you on the broad or narrow road?

Since my father had that experience, he always says that we are three in one: body, soul, and spirit. That God's Spirit is within us and that the more we live in the Spirit, our spirit gets stronger so that when we die it will be reunited with God. But if we live in the flesh, following the desires of the flesh and not showing self-control, then when we will die our spirit will go to the place reserved for people who lived in the flesh while on Earth which is hell.

Hell is real because heaven is real and my father did see heaven while in the twelve days coma. I wouldn't wish hell to my worst enemy according to what I have read from people who got visions of hell. It is time to repent and turn from our evil, selfish ways and live for God and God alone.

Maud

My experience in Israel was life changing and strengthened my relationship with the Lord Jesus Christ. A couple of weeks before the trip to Israel, the Lord had spoken to me through Isaiah 43:18–19: "Do not remember the former things, Nor consider the things of old. Behold, I will do a new thing, Now it shall spring forth; Shall you not know it? I will even make a road in the wilderness, *And* rivers in the desert."

That same week, during a Bible study, the Lord spoke through a brother in Christ stating that this trip will mark a new beginning for my family as a whole. I did not connect the dots until the day my father fell unconscious by the Jordan River. There is no word to

We were allowed to go only one by one into his room in the ICU (Intensive Care Unit). When my turn would come I would sing to Dad his favorite Christian song "Then Sings My Soul." And I would quote scriptures from the Bible to him. It was hard to see him with all these tubes coming out of his brain, of his body for his hygiene, and a big one inside his throat, etc. It was not easy to see a strong man so vulnerable. But what we didn't know is that while his body was quasi lifeless, his spirit was in heaven with God who was teaching him many things for all of us on earth.

The message that my father got from God while in the coma can be found in his book but basically it states, "Our body is the temple of the Holy Spirit, therefore let's not make our temple dirty for God is always watching and He becomes irritated when we do."

Now that my father has fully recovered within six to eight months of the incident I can really say that my father is a changed man. He is much more calm and full of wisdom.

My advice to the reader:

I am grateful that you are reading this book. By so doing, you have seen and known the pain and joy we experienced. One thing we have to keep in mind: "You never know when and how your last day will come." We have to be ready at all times, hence the question: if you were to die today, do you know where you will go? Heaven or Hell?

We are in the last days, I know this for sure every time I turn on the news. I also feel it spiritually. We must walk the talk and not just talk the talk. The road can attend more gatherings in the future—Christmas, birthdays, weddings, and childbirths.

During 12 days in the Holy Land, a bright light shined upon my mother, my three sisters, and myself, revealing to me how alive and real God is to those who call upon Him.

I pray that this book opens up your Heart to receive the Almighty as He longs to be part of your life as He is part of my family today.

Diyenat Sandie

Being in Israel during the holidays of Christmas 2010 and New Year 2011 was a life-changing experience for me. When my Dad fell down at the Jordan River due to a brain aneurysm, I did not fully understand why this was happening to us. And it was so sudden that I was just under complete shock. I could not cry and definitely I never became angry with God. I knew that God never fails and I was sure that because we were in the Holy Land, my father would not die.

I saw God's favor upon our family when we were assigned one of the best neurosurgeons in Haifa, to do the very delicate surgery on my father's brain. We also had the visit of the mother of the Israeli ambassador for Kenya, who was a complete stranger but heard of our struggles and came to support and encourage us. The outpouring of love and concerns from people abroad also gave us strength; my mother's cell phone that was roaming was constantly ringing from people who said they were praying for us.

As a family we fasted and prayed together every day for the twelve days my father was in a coma. We would visit him twice a day in the morning and late afternoon.

WHAT AN EXPERIENCE!

Individual Experiences of Our Four Daughters

Our daughters wished to contribute to this book by sharing how they lived the whole experience in Israel. In order of birth dates, here are their testimonies.

Eunice

The trip to Israel was the first time in 10 years that my family was gathering to spend Christmas together. Living in different places, my sisters and I rarely had the chance to enjoy Christmas with our parents; so the excitement was great—new country to visit, family pictures to take and stories to tell. Unexpected event happened to everyone: on December 23, 2010, at the Jordan River, my mother, sisters, and I fought death, who came claiming the life of our father.

Thinking about the days spent in that hospital in Haifa, one verse comes to my mind from Isaiah 9:2 (Amplified), "The people who walked in darkness have seen a great Light; those who dwelt in the land of intense darkness and the shadow of death, upon them had the Light shined."

I am forever grateful to the doctors, nurses, and the people of Israel who helped our family during the test of our faith. Because of their assistance, today my dad

Refrain:
Père, divin créateur
Honneur et victoire
A toi, toute la gloire!

5. Menu

   Salad
   Cucumber and thon salad
   Local kachumbari salad
   Cole slow salad
   rich salad

   Soup
   Beef with thick gravy
   Roasted chicken in coconut sauce
   Pan-fried change
   Fish bahari style

   Carving Corner
   Mbuzi tchoma with mint and chachandu

   Accompaniments
   Plain pilao
   Green banana stew

   Vegetables
   Sautéed spinach
   Vegetable stiers Chinese

   Desserts
   Cream caramel
   Cakes

b) "Thanksgiving" (Ps 126:3; Isa 25:2)

> Chorus:
> The Lord has done great things for us
> And we are glad.
>
> Stanza:
> Lord, at the Jordan River
> You made us shiver
> Eventually you gave us laughter
> For you made a city a ruin
> A fortified city a ruin.
>
> Chorus (French):
> Dieu a fait de grandes choses pour nous
> Nous nous en réjouissons

c) "Qui Est Semblable A Toi?" (Esaïe 46)

> Tu as annoncé
> Ce qui devait arriver
> Tu l'as dit et réalisé
> Tu l'as conçu et exécuté
> Qui est semblable à toi?
>
> Refrain:
> Nul n'est semblable à toi (4x)
> Oui, car tu es Dieu (4x)
>
> Tu as annoncé
> Ce qui devait arriver
> Tu l'as dit et réalisé
> Tu l'as conçu et exécuté
> Qui est semblable à toi?

être humain, la mort programmée par le Créateur depuis la chute en Eden ; je connais l'implacabilité des statistiques pour cette affection et je n'ai aucun pouvoir de placer tel malade ou tel autre dans le tiers satisfaisant. Et j'avais l'obligation pendant tout le processus le devoir de donner un point de vue devant chaque signe d'espoir ou de désespoir. Est-ce que j'avais le droit de mentir ou de dire une certaine vérité (et laquelle d'ailleurs !) quoiqu'il en soit ?

A la vérité Dieu a écouté toutes les prières et a vu le désespoir de la femme, des enfants, des amis, des frères et sœurs des communautés ecclésiales, de la famille et Il a montré son grand amour pour tous ceux qui Lui font confiance. Ce fut un grand séisme pour la vie de ce couple. Et ce doit être aussi un grand témoignage pour tous et notamment pour ceux qui n'avaient pas perdu espoir et mis leur confiance dans le pouvoir de Dieu. En effet, le Seigneur est seul capable d'accomplir une telle prouesse. AMEN!

J'ai été convaincu, comme beaucoup, que Dieu maîtrisant toutes les situations, Il ne pouvait se taire et Il a fait concourir toutes choses bonnes pour mon frère Pascal et Il va transformer cette famille.

AHUSHA, 25 Juin 2011

4. Songs of Praise

Below are the songs that we sang as a family, the lyrics and music of which were given to me by the Lord.

a) "Make a Joyful Shout to the Lord" (Ps 66:1–2)

> Make a joyful shout to God, all the earth (3x)
> Sing out the honor of his name.
> Make all his praise glorious (3x)
> Say to God,
> "How awesome are your works."

artériel. Un faible pourcentage survit à ce type d'accident et j'ai vécu cette situation depuis le début sur trois plans : en tant que neurochirurgien donc connaissant parfaitement la question, en tant que chrétien et comme membre de la famille. J'étais donc tout le temps sollicité pour donner un avis. J'ai dû puiser jusque dans mes lointains souvenirs pour tenter chaque fois de ne pas semer le désespoir autour de moi.

Mes pensées m'ont tour à tour projeté au temps de ma formation, de mon cheminement avec le Seigneur et des rapports personnels en tant que humain et parent.

Je me souvenais du dernier cours à la Faculté de médecine lorsqu'on nous annonçait que nous perdrions tous nos malades. Que nous allions sans doute les sortir des situations difficiles une fois, trois ou quatre fois mais il arrivera un jour où il faudra se résoudre qu'on aura fait ce qu'on pouvait. En d'autres termes, étant mortels, la médecine restera impuissante quand l'heure du départ aura sonné.

Dans le cas de Pascal, les statistiques étant implacables : 50% arrivent au centre de soins déjà morts et sur les 50% qui arrivent vivants, un tiers décèdent quoi qu'on fasse, un autre tiers survivra avec de lourdes séquelles et le tiers restant avec des séquelles plus ou moins importantes. Voilà donc le tableau que j'avais en face de moi en cette période d'entre deux grandes fêtes de fin d'année.

Le neurochirurgien n'avait rien de tangible pour changer le cours de l'histoire que vivaient la famille Mabika et les apparentés. C'était au tour du chrétien de prendre la relève. Cette parole de Jésus ; « si tu crois tu verras la gloire de Dieu » est vite dite lorsqu'il s'agit d'autres personnes. Quand on est soi-même impliqué et concerné, cette parole parait lointaine. Le désespoir ici est si grand qu'il l'emporte. Alors quelle demande faire à Celui qui peut tout ? Sinon, que sa volonté soit faite, qu'Il écoute ma prière ainsi que celles des autres ? Mais on se sent si désespéré, si impuissant que cette prière manque de force

En tant que parent, toutes les questions difficiles convergeaient vers moi. Je devais dire ce que j'en pensais et c'était un peu comme si on m'enfonçait le poignard dans le cœur. Je connais la finalité de chaque

2. My Message of Thanksgiving

Thanksgiving to the Lord for Pascal's Life

Father, we thank you for the family you gave us
We thank you for the plans you made for us
We thank you for sending us to Israel,
at a time set by you
We thank you for the Jordan River
It got us wet all over
We thank you for the ailment you disclosed
We thank you for the knowledge you opposed
We thank you for the divine sleep Pascal slipped into
We thank you for the dark hour we went through
We thank you for the light you showed us
that guided us all the way through
We thank you, father, for the breakthrough
We thank you for the new life you brought forth
We thank you for the new man you have wrought
Glory be to You!
Glory be to Your name!

3. Message of Thanksgiving by Daphtone MBouyou (written in French)

Mon Temoignage à La Fete D'action de grâce Pour Pascal-Bytine

Le 25 Juin 2011, une date inoubliable pour cette famille dont les membres ont connu une longue angoisse la veille de Noël 2010 en Israël, un pays étranger. Comment j'ai vécu personnellement cette situation et quel témoignage pourrai-je donner?

Pascal au cours d'un séjour touristique en famille a fait un accident vasculaire cérébral de type hémorragique par rupture d'un anévrysme

18:45–18:50	Opening Prayer (Pastor Baltazar)
18:50–19:05	Praise and Worship (Dominion Team)
19:05–19:10	Recognition of Guests (Tolu Olowoye)
19:10–19:30	Testimony by Léontine Mabika
19:30–19:40	Praise Song led by Léontine Mabika
19:40–19:50	Lifting of Glasses [Note: The more appropriate term is *toasting*.] to the Lord and Cutting of Cake (Justine Ndongo-Keller)
19:50–19:55	Thanksgiving Remarks: Eunice Mabika
19:55–21:00	Dinner (Music by Dominion Team)
21: 00–21:05	Worship Song (Led by Mrs. Judith Akwera)
21:05–21:20	Viewing of Video (c/o Eunice Mabika)
21:20–22:00	Sharing: Pascal Mabika
22:00–22:05	Worship Song: Mabika Family
22:05–22:20	Word of Exhortation: Apostle Trice Shumbusho
22:20–22:40	Thanksgiving Song and Dance: Rwanda and Democratic Republic of Congo
22:40–22:50	Thanksgiving Remarks • Roland Amoussouga, UNICTR Representative • Bishop John Shumbusho, UNICTR Christian Fellowship
22:50–23:00	Thanksgiving Song and Dance: Cameroon and Nigeria
23:00–23:10	Thanksgiving Remarks • D. & J. Mutiga and Mary Lukwago, Family Life Ministry (Nairobi)
23:10–23:15	Thanksgiving Song and Dance: Tanzania
23:15–23:30	Word of Prophecy and Blessings: Pastor Charles Akwera
23:30–23:40	Thanksgiving Remarks • Mr. and Mrs. MBouyou • Léontine Mabika
23:40–00:40	Thanksgiving Song and Dance: Congo-Brazzaville Music and Dance to the Lord Closing Prayer

leadership of my pastor and his wife, as well as my dear Sister Edith as leader of the praise-and-worship team, Sister Tolu as the master of ceremony, Pastor Mayunga as the Swahili interpreter, and Brother Aatsa as the English interpreter for Pascal, who addressed the guests in French to give the testimony of what the Lord had revealed to him while he was in coma. Many attendees from other countries gathered and performed songs and dances and read poems in honor of God for the great things and the miracle he had done, such as Rwanda, Democratic Republic of Congo, Cameroon, Tanzania, and Congo-Brazzaville.

This thanksgiving session was a memorable event in Arusha. Many Muslim friends that we had invited were really touched by the love and the power of God through our testimony and talked about what they heard at the ceremony to many other people. During the ceremony, ministers of God spoke and blessed the guests with edifying messages. My family and I, including Yaya and Durneld, sang songs and gave a testimony of what the Lord had done for us in Israel. Our desire was to heartily thank God before God himself and before men for who he was in our lives and for the great and wonderful things that he had done for us a family in Israel. Below are some items relating to the thanksgiving ceremony in Arusha.

1. Program

Programme of Thanksgiving – Mabika Family
25 June 2011
Corridor Springs Hotel

Master of Ceremonies: Tolu Olowoye
Interpreter: Pastor Mayunga

18:00–18:30   Arrival of guests
18:30–18:35   Welcome Remarks (Tolu Olowoye)
18:35–18:45   Entrance of Mabika Couple

grateful. The celebration gathered many brothers and sisters in Christ, such as Mama Maggie, Pastor Randolph and Evelyne Tebbs, Debra, UNICTR Christian Fellowship members, such as Sister Tolu, Brother George, Chantal, just to mention a few. Many people took the floor to thank God and to give their testimonies of our lives, especially the ministers of God. We received words of encouragement and, above all, words of prophecy. We were moved and greatly thankful. May the Lord bless and keep our home-fellowship family!

Thanksgiving to the Lord
June 25, 2011

On June 25, Pascal, our daughters, and I decided to organize a thanksgiving celebration in Arusha. Many friends supported us in this idea, particularly Bishops Trice and John Shumbusho, who even contributed significantly to the financial and practical arrangements of this event, as well as Chantal and her husband, Leon. Yaya and Durneld traveled from Sweden, where they had been on a field mission; Eunice and Maud traveled respectively from Dublin and the United States to attend the event.

The thanksgiving celebration took place in the evening at Corridor Springs Hotel, a hotel belonging to the Lutheran church, and gathered over a hundred and fifty guests. These guests were, among others, ministers of God and leaders from local churches, such as Pastor Baltazar, Bishop Butha, Pastor Wottango; my church pastors, elders and members; Zion City Church bishops, elders, and members; our colleagues from the UNICTR office, Christians, Muslims, and nonbelievers, including my immediate supervisor, Roland Amoussouga, who was representing the registrar of the tribunal, Mr. Adama Dieng; ICTR Christian Fellowship; special guests from Nairobi, our dear friends and mentors in the Family Life ministry, Prof. Jane and David Mutiga; our fellow countrymen, the families of Biyo, Itsouhou-Mbadinga; and many other friends in Arusha.

I would like to mention the exceptional contributions made to the event by my church, Dominion Restoration Church, under the

Mama Muchungaji, his spouse, who led the praise and worship and had composed and sung a special song just to welcome us. It was an awesome experience in the presence of God. May the Lord continue to anoint our spiritual father and his wife, increase and empower their ministry! May the Lord remember the congregation of Dominion Restoration Church and reward their hearts for service!

Pascal stayed home for about four days before resuming office, while I had to resume the next day after our arrival. At the office, we had a lot of paperwork to do in order to comply with the administrative procedures for leave and medical leave. Pascal and I had to go to the UNICTR clinic to see Dr. Epee with all the reports and for the medical assessment of the way forward. While I fully resumed my duties at the office, Pascal resumed slowly, working mostly in the mornings and going to physiotherapy sessions in the afternoon as instructed by the neurosurgeon.

The physiotherapist in Arusha really made Pascal sweat. Every day, for at least one hour, he would make him run and play basketball with him, among other things. He would come and see Pascal at the UN gym for his exercise in order to monitor his progress and check his physical condition. At the office, I had a real battle of faith to fight. Many colleagues thought that Pascal should not be working at all and should instead claim disability and stay home. I thanked God Pascal himself insisted that he would go to the office every day to do intellectual work to keep his brain working and active. His walking in the very first few weeks was not as firm and confident as it is now. It took about two months with the physiotherapy exercises for him to start walking like anybody else. Pascal's progress was amazing, both in the body and in the mind.

During those months, our home-fellowship members organized a party to thank God for our return and for the miracle of Pascal's life. They invited a number of brothers and sisters in Christ and ministers of God—including Bishops Trice and John Shumbusho from Zion City Church and our pastors, Charles and Judith Akwera—at Mama Irma and her daughter Gloria's house, just behind our house. We were so

NEW SKIN

Return to Arusha

On March 17, 2011, we took the train from Tours straight to Paris Charles de Gaulle Airport. We spent a night at a hotel near the airport so that early the next day we could catch a flight to Addis Ababa and then to Kilimanjaro Airport in Arusha, Tanzania. It had been three months since we left Arusha. Oh! An anxious and excited delegation was waiting for us at the airport, including our daughter Diyenat, Pastor Charles and Judith Akwera, Sister Edith, and our fellow countryman Auguste, just to name a few.

The UNICTR had sent us transport to take us home. Everyone was amazed to see Pascal walking, as they had been praying for him all along. Our joy was unspeakable. There was a special feast waiting for us at home. Many friends, men and women of God, visited us home, one group after the other, just to come and celebrate with us and thank God for Pascal's life. Many times, I had to tell them this story I have put in writing and how God had seen us through.

At home, I saw Pascal moving around the house, rediscovering our family surroundings, and I was happy to notice that he had not forgotten where everything was. I thanked God very much for that. The Sunday following our arrival, we went to our church, Dominion Restoration Church. This will be a memorable Sunday in our lives. The way the church welcomed us back was amazing. The whole service was dedicated to relating our testimony and praising the Lord. How we danced! How the church danced, including Pastor Charles and

The date of the appointment came. We went to the hospital. The neurosurgeon took Pascal for forty-five minutes to converse with him. Later on, he was taken for an IRM scan. By this time, Pascal was walking almost normally. Afterward, the doctor came out of his office with Pascal and indicated to me that Pascal had made considerable progress and that there was no need for them to operate Pascal for the time being. The IRM showed that despite the tiny liquid pocket, Pascal was recovering, both in his memory and physically. As a result, he allowed us to travel back to Tanzania where Pascal was to slowly resume his work and continue the physical exercises with a local physiotherapist. I lifted up the name of the Lord in praise of his faithfulness. I shared the good news with our daughters, who had been calling regularly to follow up on his progress, as a well as other relatives.

A couple of days before our return to Arusha, some of my sisters came to bid us farewell—my sister Claire from Paris, my sister Pussy and her children, my nephews, as well as my sister Chantal, also a medical doctor, from the city of Orleans. We had a wonderful family dinner at Yaya's house, and we gave thanks to the Lord for Pascal's miracle and for what the Lord had done for all of us.

take a bus and come off at the aquatic center two bus stops away. On a couple of occasions while going to the bus stop, Pascal felt unwell and fell down. People around came to help me get him up and make him sit somewhere to rest. After the swimming session, we would take the bus back home and walk again from the bus stop to the apartment.

In the house, because of his short-term memory loss, Pascal would not remember where the various rooms in the apartment were; finding the directions to the kitchen, the bathroom, or even our bedroom had become a major challenge. The apartment of Yaya and Durneld where we were staying had two levels and our bedroom was at the bottom level to make things easy for Pascal, especially in the middle of the night. But even then, Pascal would still get lost at night. I remember on several occasions, instead of going to the bathroom from our bedroom, he would open the front door, thinking that's where the toilet was. So I had to keep an eye on him every single minute.

I did not let him take his showers alone. I was always there with him, fearing that he might fall down as he did not have balance. I thanked God for Yaya and Durneld who supported me in these trying times. They were very supportive, patient, and caring. We never felt out of place, and this helped Pascal to recover quickly. May God's favor be upon them, upon their children and their children's children! Every night, before Pascal would sleep, I would put earphones to his ears to listen to the CD of the Word of God, specifically the passages spoken by Jesus Christ, which he had prepared as a Christmas gift for his daughters. He enjoyed it. Sometimes, afterward, he would continue with the songs of praise and worship brought by Gbemi and Manu.

Two months passed with the same routine. Pascal's gradual progress was noticeable. We had been given an appointment to return to the hospital to see the neurosurgeon on March 7, 2011 for an assessment of Pascal's progress. This would help the doctor decide whether Pascal would need an operation to remove the liquid in his forehead. I had been praying all this time for God to see us through.

and his wife, Dodo and Mere Okamba; Josephine; Pussy and her two boys, Harun and Joseph; and my niece Shana and her baby daughter. It was a memorable birthday, and we thanked God for having given him another year to live.

On a daily basis, for two hours, I had to take Pascal to the physiotherapist and the speech therapist. The physiotherapist's name was Florence. At the physiotherapist's office, Pascal had to undergo exercises on learning how to walk properly again. He had lost balance. At this point, he was unable to put on his trousers or tie his shoelaces alone. It was hard for him to take a step and the other. The simple walk, which we all usually take for granted, had become a major challenge for him, even standing on one leg straight or moving the arms as one does when walking. It took many, many kinesitherapy sessions for Pascal to be able to start walking slightly straight. Even then, walking fifty meters was a daunting task. He would be panting and breathless at the end. Through all Pascal's physiotherapy sessions, I was there with him, encouraging him, because some of the exercises needed considerable effort. Sometimes, Pascal would be in great pain, and I would be there to support him.

Two speech therapists worked with Pascal at the speech-therapy center owned by Mrs. Fourtouil and Mrs. Legrand. Through memory exercises given to Pascal during the sessions, it became evident that Pascal had lost his short-term memory. Mrs. Fourtouil and Mrs. Legrand would take turns in having Pascal do various types of exercises, such as mental calculations, logical games, or simple conversation to see whether he could maintain logical thinking. I was not allowed to stay with Pascal during his speech-therapy sessions. I would seize that opportunity to take a walk in the neighborhood while listening to worship songs on my MP3 player.

Twice a week, I would take Pascal to a large aquatic center in the neighborhood for Pascal to swim, as required by the doctor. I bought monthly passes for both of us. It was within walking distance. Because it was winter, Pascal could not walk for long in the cold. So we had to

Many relatives visited Pascal in the hospital, including my big sister Claire, who traveled from Paris where she had been working, to Tours to pay a visit. My uncle Ben and his wife did the same. In turns, Yaya's children and their families also came to visit. One day, we even got the visit of our daughter Maud's friends from America, Gbemi and Manu, who had come to Paris to visit another friend. Both of them drove from Paris to come and visit Pascal in hospital. They brought him a collection of praise-and-worship songs for him to listen to while alone in the hospital. Pascal's sister, Josephine, came also to visit from Lille. I thanked God we were really surrounded by family members and friends.

About three weeks later, another IRM test was run to check on the status of the tiny water pocket in Pascal's forehead. It was still there and had not changed. A college of neurosurgeons made the decision to let Pascal go home and not to operate on him immediately. They decided to give him a few weeks more to see if the water would be absorbed by itself as part of the healing process. I thanked God so much because he had heard our prayers for Pascal not to be reoperated.

Life in the House and Rehabilitation Exercises

Pascal was released from hospital on February 2, 2011. We were happy to see him home finally. However, he had to undergo daily rehabilitation exercises for kinesitherapy and orthophony. I had to contact private practitioners in our area, and thank God, the physiotherapist's office was located in the building where we were staying and the speech therapist was two buildings away. It was so practical.

We celebrated Pascal's birthday on the February 7 at a restaurant in the town center of Tours. This was Pascal's very first outing since December 23, 2010. Pascal seemed to marvel at everything. He had the look of a child discovering new things. He would see cars passing and people walking by the restaurant and would make small comments. The birthday party was attended by Yaya and Durneld; my cousin could be having a memory loss. He would not let Pascal wander about on his own in the hospital corridors. In the unit, Pascal became known as "Le Miracule' d'Israel" (the Miracle from Israel).

A number of scan and IRM tests were being run to enable the neurosurgeons to check the progress of the surgical operation done on his head and to monitor his brain. It was then that the IRM head doctor who was running the tests spoke to me in these terms: "Madam, I want you to know that your husband has come from far. We've checked the CD of what they did in Israel. It was professionally done. They did a great job. Please take good care of him. He is a real miracle." He quickly added, "He might forget one thing or another. Just remind him."

When Pascal was taken back to his ward, some other doctors came to assess Pascal's overall condition. A speech therapist was sent to Pascal's ward to run tests on him, and the result came that Pascal had lost his short-term memory. The rehabilitation exercises were therefore required. The neurosurgeon also decided that Pascal needed kinesitherapy because his walk was no longer straight, but head forward. He seemed to have lost balance.

After a few days, the result of the IRM came out. The neurosurgeon told me that the IRM had revealed that Pascal had a tiny water pocket in his forehead, and the doctors were considering the possibility of a new operation. However, they said they wanted to monitor the situation for a few weeks before taking action. When I heard this, my heart sank. I just said, "Lord please, not back there again." I dreaded the operation because he would have to be put under anesthetic again, with the possibilities of him not waking up again. My sisters and I decided to go and pray.

Weeks went by. Pascal was being observed. He had recovered his voice. I traveled to the hospital on a daily basis with a bus pass to visit him and keep him company. I would go around noon and come back home in the late evening. By now, the winter weather was at its peak. I had bought proper winter clothing.

they left with the ambulance. Pascal was taken to the ICU, where they had prepared a bed for him to spend the night so they could monitor him for a while after the long trip.

I left the hospital shortly after so Pascal could get some rest. I went to the apartment of my eldest sister and her husband, Delphine and Daphtone (known in the family as Durneld) Mbouyou. They are both retired. My sister Delphine, whom we all call Yaya, was CEO of a commercial bank before retiring in Congo-Brazzaville with her husband, a retired neurosurgeon. Yaya and Durneld have five children, all adults now with families. In my family, Yaya is the eldest of twelve—ten girls and two boys. Two among us, one girl and one boy, have gone to be with the Lord, just like our mom and dad. Durneld also happens to be the eldest of his family of nine.

Yaya and Durneld had been waiting for me, as well as some other relatives, to hear from the horse's mouth our experience in Israel. Pussy, my doctor sister, drove me to their house. It was a great family reunion. We had a very lively dinner. It was a wonderful feeling to be home and to eat homemade food. I shared the experience, notably the miracles that God did. They were really edified by it. We chatted until late and then went to bed.

The next morning, we all went to the hospital to see Pascal. I was taken to the doctor in charge while Yaya and Durneld remained to chat with Pascal. He shared with them what the spirit of God had showed him about them. Later, he was moved from the ICU to a neurology ward to wait for an empty space in the neurosurgery unit. He stayed in that ward a few days until the tracheostomy was healed. During that period, there was a lot of paperwork to be done since our medical insurance was based in Belgium and we were not affiliated to the French social security system because we were living abroad.

Time came for Pascal to be moved to the neurosurgery unit of the hospital. He was sharing a room with another patient. They became good friends. When they were alone in the room, he would spontaneously take good care of Pascal, especially when he was informed that Pascal was around 2:45 p.m. As soon as I came out of the hall of Arrivals, I switched on my Tanzanian mobile phone. It was roaming. Immediately after, our relatives called to find out whether we'd arrived and if the ambulance had come to the airport to pick us up. They said they were anxiously waiting for us at the hospital in Tours and that the ride would take about two hours because of the winter weather. I was happy to be home.

I waited for the ambulance. It came after half an hour with Pascal onboard already set for the trip. One paramedic and a driver were with us. The paramedic and I sat at the back while Pascal was lying down on a small bed. Pascal was awake. I informed him that we had arrived in France and that we had another two hours' drive before he could rest properly in the hospital. The ambulance took off for Tours.

Along the way, the paramedic and I were chatting. He would check on Pascal from time to time and ask him if he was okay or wanted anything. We tried to engage Pascal in our conversation. The back door of the ambulance had a glass window so we could see the cars right behind us driving at a higher speed on the highway. Pascal would recognize the makes of those cars and point them to us while mouthing their names. The ride took a bit longer than expected because of the rain. We reached Tours three hours later. It was already dark when we drove into the compound of the hospital. My mind was finally at rest.

Admission in Hopital Bretonneau (Tours)

The ambulance parked outside the surgery and intensive-care unit. My sister, as a medical doctor, was waiting for me at the door. We hugged for a long time. They had been praying for us to reach the hospital safely. She was very happy to see Pascal. Pascal recognized her and smiled. The paramedics carried Pascal out of the ambulance onto a bed that the nurses had brought out for him. I took my luggage out of the ambulance and carried it into one of the hospital waiting rooms, where I was told to keep it for a while. We bid farewell to the paramedics as large space where I saw my husband seated with Dr. Mayo. I was pleasantly surprised to see them there. Medical apparatuses were put in place just in case Pascal felt unwell in the air, Dr. Mayo explained to me. I found Pascal comfortably seated, a TV screen right in front of him, and Dr. Mayo was sitting next to him. He ceded his seat so I could sit next to Pascal and talk to him for a little while before takeoff. I thanked Dr. Mayo for that opportunity. I was now assured that everything was in order. So I quickly and confidently returned to my seat for takeoff.

The plane took off around eight thirty in the morning. Having slept barely two or three hours the night before, I quickly fell asleep during the flight. When I woke up, I did some reading, watched a movie, and before I knew it, we were landing at Charles de Gaulle Airport in Paris around 1:30 p.m. When the plane landed, it taxied for a long while before stopping. The flight attendants were at the door waiting for instructions to open it. Meanwhile, Dr. Mayo came to fetch me to go to the compartment where Pascal was. Then he gave me all the documents and the files for the French hospital. I was surprised, so I asked him: "Oh, you are not coming with us?" He answered, "Unfortunately, no. We are flying back to Tel Aviv after one hour."

While we were talking, three airport security men came in looking for us. I introduced myself to them and showed them our passports and explained that we had just come from Israel and that my husband was on medical transfer. Two paramedics were following them with a stretcher. Pascal was taken away on the stretcher to the ambulance that, I was told, had been allowed to come and pick him up from the plane. Before going out, I bid farewell to Dr. Mayo and profusely thanked him for all he had done for us. The airport security explained to me what I was to do—get off the plane, go through the immigration and customs formalities on my own, get all the luggage I had checked in and, exit through a specific gate to wait for the ambulance. I followed the instructions and went to the stated exit gate to wait for the ambulance.

It was very cold outside, and I had no coat. It was winter in France with all the gloom and rain, on the 13th January, when we arrived. It few explanations in Hebrew. The security was very tight. Just before these men left with Dr. Mayo, Pascal and his travelling documents, Dr. Mayo told me to go and check in our luggage and meet them later on board the plane.

As soon as I got out of the ambulance with the luggage, I saw a team member of Danny's tour company coming toward me. It was Harel. I was so happy to see him. The first and last time I had met him was in Tel Aviv, with Charity, before we started the guided tour, but we had been communicating on the phone for the changes to our return flights. He came and said he had been waiting for me to help me with the check-in and the immigration procedures. I was glad to see a familiar face. Harel helped me with the luggage to the check-in counters and then through the immigration, all the way up to the gate where I was to board the flight. I thanked him so much for being at the airport that early in the morning for me. And I also thanked the Lord for making things easy for me.

On Board Flight El Alal

While waiting to board the flight, I called our pastor, Charles Akwera, to tell him that we were now boarding the flight to France. He prayed for us and wished us a safe trip. When I boarded the flight, I was thinking it was going to be one of the airlines that I know go to Paris, such as Ethiopian Airlines or Air France. I had not been informed beforehand of the airline company or aircraft that we were going to take. As soon as I entered, I saw a few passengers to my right and was directed to the business-class compartment. Flight attendants started checking on passengers and takeoff procedures were being shown on the screens. I started looking around me to see where my husband was.

A few minutes later, the drawn curtains before me were opened and I saw a crew member beckoning me to follow him. I followed him along a corridor that I was surprised to see because I didn't realize the plane was that long. Then he opened another curtain, and I entered another

ON THE EAGLE WINGS

Medical Evacuation to Tours, France
January 13, 2011

Just after three o'clock, the ambulance reached the hospital. It was very quiet and the lights were dim, but I found a male nurse preparing my husband for the trip. He had dressed him in his own clothes, the jumper I had bought for him earlier, and some tennis shoes. He had also shaved him. They had removed the long tube from the tracheostomy and left a short one in case it had to be used again on the journey. Dr. Mayo came to join me. I took all of Pascal's belongings from the hospital, and we all went down to the ambulance. Pascal was put in a wheelchair and pushed to the lift down to the ambulance. He had no tube, no bandage, nothing showing that he was coming from a hospital. He looked so different to me. I was happy to see him that way.

As soon as we settled in the ambulance around 3:30 a.m., we took off for Tel Aviv. The drive was smooth, and we got there around five thirty. As soon as we entered the airport area, the ambulance was parked in the emergency parking area not too far from the entrance of the airport departures. As soon as the ambulance stopped and the doors opened, even before I got down from the car, security men came and asked me questions about who we were and where we were going while examining our passports. They asked me many private questions. They also turned to Pascal who was still seated in the ambulance and questioned him. They quickly realized he could not talk though he had tried to whisper something. Dr. Mayo then intervened to add a told Pascal that Eunice and I were going back to the hotel to pack and prepare for our respective trips.

After taking a short nap, we woke up to start the preparations. While I was busy making the last phone calls from Israel to the French hospital to make sure it was ready to receive Pascal and to confirm our arrival to the private ambulance company the next day at Charles de Gaulle airport, Eunice packed all our bags, mine and her father's. I was so grateful for her valuable assistance. I thanked God for my daughter Eunice. I don't know what I would've done without her there. She was that strong pillar that I leaned on during that trying time. At times, I would feel weak and she would be my strength, through her prayers, encouraging words, and her practical assistance. May the Lord lift up his countenance upon her and give her peace!

Eunice was to travel the next day as well, around eleven o'clock, and Danny's team was to assist her also with her travel arrangements. After dinner, Eunice and I went to bid farewell to the personnel of the hotel and then called Diyenat, Maud and Cap on Skype to thank God together for all that had happened in Israel and pray for journey mercies. By midnight, we switched off the lights to rest a bit for two hours until the ambulance came. The ambulance came on the dot. Eunice helped me with the suitcases to the car. I hugged my daughter to bid her farewell. My heart was heavy as I was leaving her behind on her own. But I put her in the hands of God and asked God to keep her until she returned safely to Dublin. And the ambulance drove off to the hospital.

would be fine and that we were happy to go home, to a place where we had many relatives, including medical doctors. May the Lord reward Ambassador Jacob, his spouse, and Bruria a hundredfold!

We spoke to Danny on the phone to inform him of the impending Pascal's medical evacuation. Not only he indicated that his team members would be at the airport to help me with the check-in, immigration, and security procedures, but also they would help Eunice secure a flight to Dublin on the same day as Pascal and I in the evening and provide the same assistance at the airport. What's more? He said that I should not worry about all the hotel bills we had incurred in Haifa as a result of Pascal's condition, that he would pay all of them, and that we could leave Israel with peace of mind and when we reach home, we could pay him back when ready! That was another miracle from God! May the Lord bless him and his team!

At twelve in the morning, during the visiting hours, Eunice and I went to the hospital. We found my husband seated. The nurses explained to us that he was to take the flight to Paris around eight o'clock in the morning from Haifa and that I had to prepare his travel documents and give them to Dr. Mayo, who would accompany us. That afternoon, Dr. Amsalem came to Pascal's ward to see him for the last time and bid us farewell. He indicated to us that Pascal's tracheostomy would be removed in France and recommended that all IRM and scans done to Pascal be sent to him also for his follow up. He warmly bid us farewell and left. May the Lord make his face shine upon Dr. Amsalem!

The same afternoon, Dr. Mayo came to look for me to brief me on the preparations made for Pascal's medical evacuation to France by the hospital. He advised me to bring for Pascal some warm clothes, shoes and socks for the trip and to be ready with my luggage by 3:00 am because an ambulance was to pick me up from my hotel to the hospital and pick up Pascal and himself before heading for the airport in Tel Aviv. The flight to Paris was at 8.30 am. He had with him our three tickets and he kept Pascal's passport. At the end of the visiting hour, I

The week that followed the trip to France saw remarkable progress. Pascal could now feed himself, although in the beginning, his hand would try to find where his mouth was. He could stay seated for a longer period. I would carry his laptop to the hospital and give it to him to see how he would handle it. I would put it on and see what he would do. He would try to type a word or two or open his 3D architectural software for his drawings. But after fifteen minutes or so, he would look weary. I would move to another activity. Eunice would take pictures of him trying to stand or doing some things and would show him the said pictures. Then I would call our relatives abroad while at the hospital with him and give him news or convey to him their greetings. He would respond by nodding, showing that he was in agreement. We would initiate a conversation with him. Eunice and I would do our best to read his lips in an attempt to gather his message.

Bruria came to visit again a couple of times before the date of Pascal's medical evacuation. By this time, the necessary arrangements had been made. Dr. Koirala informed me that Pascal was to leave the hospital for France on January 13, 2011. The short tracheostomy tube on Pascal would be taken care of in the French hospital. He explained to me the administrative arrangements made by the UN (the UNICTR, the UN Mission in Jerusalem, and the UN Headquarters) for Pascal's medical evacuation to France, accompanied by Dr. Mayo and me and the tickets paid for us to travel. Dr. Mayo contacted me later on to introduce himself and give some guidelines as to what to prepare for Pascal as clothing for the trip. He also wanted to know whether doctors in the receiving hospital in France could confirm that Pascal was expected, as well as the availability of the ambulance at the airport upon arrival. My sister Pussy helped us greatly in this. May the Lord bless the work of her hands!

When Bruria knew we were travelling to France for further treatment, out of love, she was a bit reluctant, indicating that she would have preferred to see Pascal complete his treatment in the Holy Land. She was concerned for us. I managed to convince her that everything bed to suck out the phlegm so that the tube could remain clean. Every time they did that exercise, I found it hard to watch.

After the visiting hour, Eunice and I went back to the hotel. It was now after 2:00 p.m. I used that afternoon to call the UN medical doctor and the chief of administration at the UNICTR for the modalities of the evacuation. I communicated the information to Dr. Koirala, although he was to go on home leave shortly before the medical evacuation. He gave me names of new contacts to liaise with for follow up, particularly with the UNICTR administration in Arusha. I had to contact and book an ambulance from the private company Ambulances Barthès Jussieu in Tours. The ambulance was to travel from Tours straight to Paris Charles De Gaulle Airport to pick up Pascal and drive him back to the Hôpital Bretonneau in Tours. I made those arrangements and also contacted our medical insurance to send a guarantee letter to the said hospital before Pascal could be evacuated there.

In the evening, after Eunice and I visited Pascal, we had a time of prayer before dinner to thank God for what he was doing in Pascal's life. At one point, while praying, the spirit of God reminded of the peeling off of Pascal's skin I had discovered in the morning and said "Why did you ask Dr. Amsalem what you saw? Didn't I tell you I would make him a new man?" It is then that my spirit opened and the revelation of what Eunice had told us earlier on, became a reality and assumed a meaning to me. I shared the insight with Eunice and we both burst out into thanksgiving to the Lord even more for his faithfulness.

The administrative machine was a bit slow, and sometimes I had to write a lot of emails left and right to the UNICTR management, to the medical unit of the UN Mission in Jerusalem, and to the hospital in France, providing information that one of them or the other needed. It was taxing, but I thanked God things were on the right track. Dr. Koirala had made arrangements with the hospital administration to find out the doctor who would accompany Pascal on the medical evacuation. His name was Dr. Mayo. Dr. Mayo and I worked closely on this evacuation to finalize the arrangements.

On January 7, in the morning, I attended to Pascal being given his first bath since he came out of the coma. I was with the nurses, and I helped them to take Pascal to the shower. When Pascal was undressed, what I saw on his body was unbelievable. From the neck down, huge chunks of his skin were peeling off all over his body. I had never seen anything like that before. I asked the nurses what this was due to. They responded that it would be better to ask the doctor. I helped Pascal, who could barely stand in the shower, soap his body. With a sponge, I helped to scrub off all the old skin and applied a lot of body lotion to moisturize the body.

In the course of the day, when Dr. Amsalem came to visit Pascal, that was the question I asked him. "Why is his body peeling off so much?" Dr. Amsalem examined Pascal's body, and by the look on his face, I could tell he was also doubtful. The only thing he said was, "You know, Mrs. Mabika, the most important thing is for Pascal to be alive. All the rest is just a matter of aesthetics." I understood what he meant. So I left it at that. He indicated that Pascal was to have his first meal through the mouth that lunchtime and that we should start slowly to see how he would react, then later on leave Pascal to eat for himself. The food was not to be solid and had to be in small quantities. Even the water had to be given to him through a straw. Whenever Dr. Amsalem came, it was just to have a small chat with Pascal and see how he was behaving. Obviously, Pascal could not respond as he was voiceless. Dr. Amsalem reassured me that when the tracheostomy would be healed and the tube removed, we would be able to hear his voice.

The nurse would come and bring Pascal's food, and I would help her feed Pascal slowly. After Pascal had eaten, they would try to make him sit on a multipurpose chair for digestion, and whenever they wanted to change him, they would pull up the tray that would bring out two metal rods for Pascal to hold on to while trying to stand up. From time to time, Pascal would cough violently, and the phlegm in his throat would come out through the tube connected through the tracheotomy. The nurses would use a small machine that was in the room next to his of God." They danced while waving the flags to the music. And from time to time, one person would lift his or her voice to praise and worship God. The music was sweet. The atmosphere was Spirit-filled.

At one point, I spontaneously stood up to lift my voice and worship God. I cried all my heart to God in thanksgiving. I had all reasons to praise him. His answers to our prayers, his guidance, his provision, his faithfulness, his love for us, the miracle he had just done for Pascal, bringing him out of a coma, all came to my mind. Tears fell from my eyes. I thanked him for having taken us to that unique service, thus allowing my daughter and I to see and experience such an exceptional time in his presence. It was refreshing and unforgettable!

At the end of the service, Colleen introduced us to the lady pastor of the church (her husband was away on mission) as well as to her family and other church leaders. We were warmly surrounded. Many people came to meet us to comment on the miracle that the Lord had performed and praise his name. The pastor and Colleen took some pictures of us. The pastor gave us a CD of their songs. We were very thankful. Thereafter, Colleen drove us back to our hotel. By the time we reached it, it was time for dinner.

Arrangements for Medical Evacuation

It was later decided that Pascal could not be evacuated to Arusha, our duty station, as it lacked medical facilities, but to France, our home country and place of home leave.

Dr. Koirala started liaising with the UNICTR management for the practical arrangements of the medical evacuation to France. In the meantime, I managed to get the name of the French hospital as well as the names of the doctors who would receive Pascal and whom the doctors in Haifa would communicate with for medical reports and for further feedback. While those arrangements were undergoing, I continued to take care of Pascal.

the other doctor who spoke with my sister for him to discuss with them, gather information, and inform our employer accordingly. While he had gone to meet the doctors, Colleen came back to visit us at the hospital. She was pleasantly surprised to see what the Lord had done for us. We held a short conversation. She informed us that in the afternoon that day at 4:00 p.m, they would be having a praise service in church and that if we wanted to attend, she could come and pick us later in the afternoon at our hotel. We agreed. Eunice and I thanked her and indicated that we would be waiting for her at the hotel. Then she left after promising to inform her pastor and church leaders accordingly.

Dr. Koirala came back later on and informed us of what was in the pipeline. He indicated that they had decided to keep Pascal in the hospital for another week to monitor him before he could travel on medevac and that in the meantime he would be discussing with the UN authorities in Arusha, Tanzania, and in the headquarters to determine where and how to evacuate him.

At the appointed time, Colleen came to pick us up at the Colony Hotel and drove us to her church. The church was located on a hill, Mount Carmel, in the city of Haifa, and it was called Kehilat HaCarmel. This is a community of Messianic believers, whose vision is to restore the altar of the Lord on Mount Carmel based on 1 Kings 18:30. Eunice and I were amazed by the way it was built—on a hill and surrounded by twelve big stones representing the twelve tribes of Israel.

When we were taken inside, we saw that the altar was flooded with light coming through the glass roof right above it. It was a beautiful scene! We were welcomed in and taken straight to sit on the altar where the leaders of the church were seated. The female pastor of the church was leading the praise and worship while playing the piano. I've never heard such soft and beautiful songs in Hebrew. Some were in English. The lyrics of the songs were being projected on a screen.

As the congregation was praising and worshipping, standing, some ladies entered the church with flags of different colors, on which were written "King of kings" or "Lord of lords" or "Son of God" or "Lamb

Out of the Intensive Care Unit

The medics installed Pascal at the other end of the ward, next to its door, and blocked his bed there. They adjusted the tracheostomy tube under his collarbone and connected it to some machine that would be activated from time to time to suck Pascal's sputum whenever he coughed. Pascal was now in an ordinary ward. No more permanent lights. No more noise of breathing machines! What a relief! What a peace! It was kind of normal life. We felt good.

Then another visitor arrived, Bruria, accompanied by her assistant. She was jubilant when she got the news. She had a powerful voice and spoke with a lot of confidence. We conversed for a good while, and Bruria left. The visiting hour came to an end. Danny, Eunice, and I bid farewell to Pascal and left. We went to a restaurant to have lunch.

At the restaurant, Danny was amazing. He treated us as his family members. We had an informative conversation about the Holy Land, his family, as well as his business, which takes him many places, including East Africa. We had a nice lunch and spent a wonderful time together. Then he dropped us at our hotel and departed.

Back at the hotel, I called my sister Lucie, nicknamed by the family as Pussy. She was a medical doctor, an anesthetist in the regional hospital center of Tours known as Hôpital Bretonneau. She had requested me to send Pascal's IRM CDs to enable her and her colleagues in the relevant medical units to see what had happened and the progress being made. When she heard that Pascal had emerged out of coma, she requested to speak to one of the doctors in the ICU. I met the social welfare lady in the hospital and explained to her the situation. She put me in contact with another doctor who could also speak French and was therefore able to explain medically to my sister what had been done on Pascal and what they were planning to do before they could send him anywhere on medical evacuation for further treatment.

Around January 6, 2011, Dr. Koirala came to the hospital to see us. After checking on Pascal, I introduced him to the ICU head doctor and them also. He promised to drive back to Haifa to see us. Bruria was very happy. She said she would pass by as quickly as possible.

I called the management of the tribunal, namely the registrar, the chief of administration, and the UN medical doctor, to tell them what had happened. I added that Dr. Koirala had promised to drive again from Jerusalem to see us and speak with the doctors in order to know the way forward. We decided to inform our relatives in France, in the United States of America, and in Congo-Brazzaville, as well as our friends wherever they were, in Tanzania, Kenya, Dublin, etc. We received many phone calls that day, people shouting of joy and rejoicing with us over the phone. It was a unique day in our lives!

Back at Colony Hotel, Eunice and I decided to go for a late lunch to a restaurant nearby and then walked to a mall in the neighborhood for the first time. We did some shopping. I bought a pair of boots and some jumpers and two nice pullovers for my husband.

The next day, Eunice and I went to visit Pascal at 11:00 a.m as usual. We found him seated, supported by pillows. He had less tubes and drips. When we went in, he turned his head toward us with a familiar look. Eunice quickly said, "Dad is really awake. I recognize that look in his eyes." We greeted him and teased him. He would smile and murmur something. He was still voiceless. The nurse told us they had him stand out of bed and take a few steps earlier that morning. She said the progress was good and they were intending that morning to take him out the ICU to a normal ward.

Danny was announced to me. I went to meet him outside and took him to see Pascal while Eunice went to wait outside. I introduced him to Pascal. Pascal nodded and smiled at him. He was delighted to meet Pascal for the very first time. We chatted for a short while. Then the nurse came to tell us that two medics had come to take Pascal and move him to another ward outside. They took him and his bed and pushed him out along the corridor into another ward, where we found a patient with his relatives, conversing.

I called the ICU later that evening to check how Pascal was doing. The first time, I was told he had closed his eyes and had gone back to "sleep" and the nurse was monitoring him. In my heart and my spirit, I was repeatedly telling God "He is just sleeping...he will reopen his eyes." At this time, my phone rang. It was Danny! I was happy to hear from him. He said he has just arrived in Haifa and wondered whether he could see Pascal and us. I told him we would be delighted to see him again, so we agreed to meet at Rambam Hospital the day after next during our visiting hours and thereafter go for a bite.

In the morning, when we went to the hospital, we found Pascal still lying down but awake. He looked at us when we went in. The nurse in the ICU now knew us and spoke to us often. She would also do us a favor by letting Eunice and I come in at the same time so that we could try to hold a conversation with Pascal. The big tube in the mouth had been removed and had been replaced by a tracheostomy tube running from below his chin to a machine outside. His mouth was now free. He could murmur something, but he had no voice because his vocal cords had been disconnected. He was breathing on his own. What a miracle!

We told him how happy we were that he was awake. We informed him what we had been doing, what day it was, and the fact that Diyenat, Maud, and Capucine had travelled back. We gave him news of our relatives and friends who had been calling to find out how he had been doing. From time to time, he would nod and try to say something. We would manage to read his lips to try to understand him and respond. The one-hour visit went by fast. We kissed him good-bye, and while following us with his eyes, he managed to lift his right hand and wave at us when we stood at the door of his ward. We waved back and left.

Outside the ICU, Eunice and I were commenting on what the Lord had done. We were so happy. We felt light as if we had been relieved of a heavy burden. We felt like we had wings. We called Diyenat, Maud, and Cap to break the great news to them. We promised to talk to them on Skype later that night. I called Dr. Koirala and Bruria to inform

"This time I will not be ashamed." I was convinced deep down that this time was the right time. I waved my hand in front of Pascal's face, and he blinked. Everyone around saw this. Then I decided to move away from him to see if his eyes would follow my movement. I walked around his bed, and I noticed his eyes were following me.

The head doctor wanted more proof. She said, "Speak to him, say something, for us to see if he can hear you."

I walked back near his head and spoke to him in our Congolese language. I told him, "People are waiting to see if you can hear my voice. Do something with any part of your body to show us that you hear me and understand what I mean." He moved slightly his right middle finger. Everybody around the bed was convinced now that he was awake and could understand. My joy was indescribable. I nearly cried.

As I was leaving the ward full of joy with the other nurses, I saw Dr. Amsalem coming from the other end of the corridor. He hurried toward us with his arms wide open saying, "Mrs. Mabika, you see, Pascal has awakened!' I hugged him in joy. He explained to me that he was intending to remove the big tube that was in Pascal's mouth and replace it with a tracheotomy to help him breathe. When I heard that, I got concerned because in my mind came immediately the specter of another surgical operation. He saw the expression on my face and quickly explained to me that it was a minor operation and that he would actually do it right where Pascal was. Then we parted ways. I learned later on that Dr. Amsalem had really fought to keep Pascal connected to the machines in the hope that he would wake up one day.

Eunice and I returned to the hotel rejoicing. When we got back to Colony Hotel, we announced to the receptionists who had been inquiring about Pascal's condition that he had awakened. They shared our joy, and with a smile on their faces, they said, "We told you it would be okay." Back to our room, Eunice and I burst into thanksgiving and singing to God. We decided to wait until the next day after the first visit to the hospital to break the news to our relatives, family friends, and church community who had been supporting us in prayer.

THE MIRACLE

God's Miracle

On January 4, 2011, Eunice and I took a bus for the hospital. We visited Pascal. His condition had not changed. We returned in the evening. As we were taking turns to go inside, Eunice went in first and I stayed outside behind the ICU door.

Immediately after she entered, I heard Eunice scream, "Mommy! Mommy!" My heart sank. My first thought was he was gone—my daughter did not find her father there because they had disconnected him from the machines and taken him away. Instinctively, I forced the ICU door open and ran inside Pascal's room. Even the guard was startled and also followed suit. I met Eunice coming out with her eyes wide open. Before I had a chance to ask what was wrong, she screamed, "Mommy, Dad has opened his eyes!"

I rushed to my husband's bedside. Behold, I saw his eyes were *wide open*! I looked at his eyes, and I could not believe my own eyes. My heart was racing in my chest. The other nurses in the unit came in to see. I quickly ran to the office of the head doctor of the ICU. I told her, "My husband's eyes are open!" She said, "Yes, I'm coming with you." She followed me to my husband's ward and told me to do something as if to find out he was really awake.

Before I did anything, a Bible verse from one of the psalms (and I did not remember then which one) quickly came into my mind, saying, "Those who look up onto the Lord, their faces will be radiant, and they will not be covered with shame." I responded to the Spirit, whispering, that she was an amazing woman who had traveled a great deal to and within Africa and had been among the very first young people to come and pray for the sick in Rambam Hospital. That practice spread, and she became known.

Eunice and I went back to the hotel. In the evening, we visited Pascal again. One after the other, we prayed, read to him the Bible verses that the Spirit had told us to go and read to him that day, and sang songs of praise to his ears. By this time, the nurse inside the ward had known us. We had become familiar to most of the nurses and the social welfare lady at the ICU. When we went back to the hotel that evening, I was feeling tired and weak physically. I took a shower and went immediately to bed to rest, while Eunice was completing an assignment for her office.

where they caught their flights early morning on the third. My firstborn, Eunice, who was working in Dublin, had decided to stay. She did not want to leave me alone under such circumstances. She called her employer to explain the situation. They came to the agreement that her office would send her work by email and she could work from Haifa to make it possible for her to stay with me. I profusely thanked God for that favor and for Eunice! I was very grateful for that touch of love.

On January 3, 2011, in the morning, Eunice and I went to the hospital. Pascal was still in a coma. We went to read the Word of God to him, and as the Lord had instructed me, I touched his whole body again with my two hands, pleading with the Spirit to breathe life back into him. During that visiting hour, one nurse came to tell me that someone wanted to see me. I was really wondering who it could be. I went out, and I saw a woman on a wheelchair being pushed by another lady.

The woman was elderly and was very elegant. As soon as she saw Eunice and me, she opened her arms and said, "Here you are! I've been looking for you!" and then she hugged us. "My name is Bruria. Jacob, my son-in-law, told me what happened to you. I've come to visit."

This lady seemed to be well known in the hospital. Everyone passing by knew her and greeted her. The people in the hospital were surprised to see that she knew us. Eunice and I were wondering who she was, as she seemed popular.

After all the greetings, she said to us, "Are you okay? Sorry about what happened. What can I do for you? Which hotel are you staying at?"

We answered, "Colony Hotel."

And she went on, "Are you okay? Have you been eating fine? What can I do for you? Please feel free to ask me anything. I can give you anything...except, of course, life to your husband."

In my heart, I was thanking God to meet such a person who was so ready and so willing to do everything to help us. We chatted for a while. After we exchanged contact details, she made sure Eunice and I had an appointment with her for dinner at her residence one evening. We were meant to go there the following night. We later found out

She then told me that the scan would take place around 1:00 p.m. and if I waited, I could go with the medics to accompany him. I came out of her office and joined my daughters outside. They were all anxious to know what the doctor had said. I related to them our conversation. We waited in the family waiting room. In the meantime, we prayed hard, asking God not to allow this third operation. My prayer was for the scanner not to show anything wrong and whatever the case would be, there wouldn't be need for a third operation.

Time for the scanner came. The medics arrived and pushed my husband's bed outside the ICU to go to the IRM unit. IRM, an abbreviation for Imagerie à résonance médicale, is a French medical term that could be translated as medical resonance imaging When we got there, they told me to wait outside in the corridor and went in. I waited outside. I continued to pray asking God to intervene. Some half an hour later, they came out with a CD and took my husband straight back to the ICU. This time, I could not go back in with them because the visiting hour had elapsed. I wondered how I was going to get to know the results of the scan before the next visiting hour.

Oh, God is good! On the way back to the hotel, the phone in my bag rang. I quickly picked the call. It was Dr. Amsalem, informing me that the scanner had not shown anything wrong and that nothing had changed since the operation. He was happy with the results, just as my daughters and I were. We went back to the hotel with a feeling of having grown wings as we felt encouraged that the Lord had heard us and answered our prayer. That evening in the hospital, Diyenat, Maud, and Cap bid farewell to their father as time had come for them to go back to their respective countries for their various occupations. In fact, they had no choice since they had already overstayed their authorized leave. With the assistance of Vered H. Tour, we managed to rebook them on new flights and paid penalties where it was required.

My daughters left that day, first, Diyenat to Kilimanjaro, through Addis and Nairobi, in the evening, and Maud and Cap to the United States later in the night. They took the train from Haifa to Tel Aviv, duties as protocol and external-relations officer. I was shocked to see him there. He explained to me that he had come to visit us after he had been informed by Danny, the manager of Vered H. Tour, of my husband's condition and since he was in Israel for official business, he had driven from Jerusalem to Haifa to come and see us.

I introduced him to my daughters and sincerely thanked him so much for having taken the time, despite his tight schedule, to pay us a visit at the hospital. I was very much moved by his kindness. And I was also grateful to God for having sent to us a person we knew. I took him inside the ward to see my husband. He came out after a few minutes, and we continued discussing. After a short while, His Excellency took my mobile number and informed me that he would make sure that his mother-in-law who lived in Haifa get in touch with us in case we needed anything. Then he left.

The Battle of Faith

I went back into the ICU. The head doctor of the unit expressed that she wanted to talk to me. I followed her to her office. My heart was pounding in my chest, knowing that whenever I heard from her, it was something serious. She said that they were intending to take my husband for another scan to check what was wrong and if the scans showed anything, they would have to reoperate him immediately. Here, she presented me with some papers to sign as consent for the third operation.

Spontaneously, I said out loud to myself, "No! There can't be another operation! If he has not woken up after the first two, what's going to happen after the third one!"

The doctor caught my thoughts and asked, "You don't agree with what we're planning?"

I said, "Not really. Let's first wait for the new scan, and we would decide accordingly."

he not do it? or hath he spoken, and shall he not make it good?

Numbers 23:19

Heaven and earth shall pass away, but my words shall not pass away.

Matthew 24: 35

After reading these scriptures, I touched his body, as the voice had commanded, where I could. It was covered here and there by one apparatus or another. I massaged his toes, his fingers, and his face, while calling upon the Spirit to quicken it back to life. After fifteen minutes, my daughters took their turns to go in and read their verses. Then we went back to the hotel. On the way back, I felt peace.

We went to rest in our rooms. While dozing off, like in a dream, I heard a message whisper to my ear, "This time, when you go to the hospital, you sing to his ears songs of praise." When I woke up late afternoon, I confidently told my daughters that in the evening, during our visit, we would take turns singing softly to Pascal's ear songs of praise. We all chose songs that we knew he liked and usually played on the guitar. I sang one Congolese song that we used to sing some years back when we were still in the youth group of our church in Congo, "Nge Mfumu Kena ma Nzulu, Tala beto Kena kudila Nge" ("You God in Heaven See and Hear Our Cry"), and the songs "Lord I Lift Your Name on High" and "Be Glorified." Afterward, I touched again his whole body with my hands, requesting the Spirit to breathe life into it.

The next day, January 2, when we went back to the hospital in the morning, while I was visiting Pascal in the intensive care unit, the social welfare lady came in to tell me that someone outside in the corridor wanted to see me. When I went out, I couldn't believe who was standing there waiting for me. It was the ambassador of Israel to Kenya. I had previously met him at the UNICTR in the course of my

I went in first. Pascal's body was still lifeless. I noticed his whole body had really swollen. I found they had repositioned him to lie sideways. His eyes were smeared with ointment, and I asked the nurse why they were like that. The nurse responded that it was to prevent his eyelids from blocking. I had taken the habit of talking to my husband to give him news of the family, what we were doing and how we were expecting him to come to be well so we could go back. Here are some of the promises of God that I read softly to him:

> Thou hast granted me life and favour, and thy visitation hath preserved my spirit.
>
> Job 10:12

> Many are the afflictions of the righteous: but the Lord delivereth him out of them all. He keepeth all his bones: not one of them is broken.
>
> Psalms 34:19–20

> And the prayer of faith shall save the sick, and the Lord shall raise him up; and if he have committed sins, they shall be forgiven him.
>
> James 5:15

> Who his own self bare our sins in his own body on the tree, that we, being dead to sins, should live unto righteousness: by whose stripes ye were healed.
>
> 1 Peter 2:24

> God is not a man, that he should lie; neither the son of man, that he should repent: hath he said, and shall

people, I will open your graves, and cause you to come up out of your graves, and bring you into the land of Israel. And ye shall know that I am the Lord, when I have opened your graves, O my people, and brought you up out of your graves, And shall put my spirit in you, and ye shall live, and I shall place you in your own land: then shall ye know that I the Lord have spoken it, and performed it, saith the Lord.

Ezekiel 37: 1–14

I repeatedly told God that His Spirit was in my husband and that the dry bones of my husband would live.

God's Directions

My time of prayer came to an end. Around six thirty, I went to the bathroom to have a shower before going back to bed to rest. While I was having the shower, I heard a voice tell me, "When you go to the hospital today, take your Bible and go and read to your husband all my promises that you know. When you finish, you touch his body with your hands." And the voice went quiet. I was startled. I thought it was my mind playing tricks on me. After the shower, I went back to the room and lay down on the bed to rest a bit while waiting for my daughters to wake up. I was thinking about what I had just heard, wondering whether it was the fruit of my imagination. Then a Bible verse came quickly into my mind from Psalm 32: 8 "I will instruct thee and teach thee in the way which thou shalt go: I will guide thee with mine eye." I made up my mind—I was going to obey.

When time came for us to go to the hospital, I shared with my daughters what happened and the message I heard. I was very glad they were supportive. Each one of us prepared our own biblical passages to go and read to Pascal. Only I was to touch his body. When we arrived, as usual, we went inside one after the other.

something. That particular night, I focused my prayer time on the book of Ezekiel, the chapter relating to the valley of dry bones.

> The hand of the Lord was upon me, and carried me out in the spirit of the Lord, and set me down in the midst of the valley which was full of bones, And caused me to pass by them round about: and, behold, there were very many in the open valley; and, lo, they were very dry. And he said unto me, Son of man, can these bones live? And I answered, O Lord God, thou knowest. Again he said unto me, Prophesy upon these bones, and say unto them, O ye dry bones, hear the word of the Lord. Thus saith the Lord God unto these bones; Behold, I will cause breath to enter into you, and ye shall live: And I will lay sinews upon you, and will bring up flesh upon you, and cover you with skin, and put breath in you, and ye shall live; and ye shall know that I am the Lord. So I prophesied as I was commanded: and as I prophesied, there was a noise, and behold a shaking, and the bones came together, bone to his bone. And when I beheld, lo, the sinews and the flesh came up upon them, and the skin covered them above: but there was no breath in them. Then said he unto me, Prophesy unto the wind, prophesy, son of man, and say to the wind, Thus saith the Lord God; Come from the four winds, O breath, and breathe upon these slain, that they may live. So I prophesied as he commanded me, and the breath came into them, and they lived, and stood up upon their feet, an exceeding great army. Then he said unto me, Son of man, these bones are the whole house of Israel: behold, they say, Our bones are dried, and our hope is lost: we are cut off for our parts. Therefore prophesy and say unto them, Thus saith the Lord God; Behold, O my

the tribunal. Dr. Koirala really followed closely with the medics my husband's progress. It was reassuring to have him with us. May God bless the work of his hands and his family!

On the thirtieth, when we returned to the hospital, I found my husband's eyes had slightly opened. I was excited, thinking he had started waking up. I told the nurse, and she said it was good and I might want to go see the doctor in charge. I ran to that office, happily telling her, "I saw my husband's eyes slightly opened. I think he's waking up." But she told me otherwise, reiterating that there was no life in him and that it was just a reflex and that we could walk back to see him so I could understand what she was talking about. When we reached my husband's bed, I waved my hand in front of his eyes to see if he could blink, but his eyelids did not move at all. And the doctor returned quickly back to her office after telling me, "I told you so!'

By this time, discouragement had started settling in. The receptionist at our hotel became concerned because he had not seen us take breakfast or lunch. He wondered what was going on. He was very positive. He told us a couple of times, "Please do not be discouraged. It will be okay. It is not for nothing that this incident has happened in Israel." We would thank him for his positive mind and encouraging words.

On the night of the December 31, we broke our fast around six o'clock and we went for dinner outside for two hours and came back indoors. New Year's Eve party was in full swing, and the street along our hotel was crowded and very bright with festive lights. We finished praying, and one of us continued for the chain prayer, while the rest went to bed. When it was my turn at 4:00 a.m., I woke up to pray. I spoke to God in these terms: "Lord, time is passing, and nothing is happening. I'm feeling tired in the body, in the mind, and in the spirit. There is no way my husband can go back to Arusha in a coffin. What type of testimony would that be while visiting the Holy Land? We have now overstayed our planned time in Israel, and we have to change six tickets and pay all the penalties. We have no idea how long we're going to be here. The hotel bills are piling up…" I pleaded with God to do

Lord, with the favour that thou bearest unto thy people: O visit me with thy salvation; That I may see the good of thy chosen, that I may rejoice in the gladness of thy nation, that I may glory with thine inheritance.

Psalms 106:1–5

No man putteth a piece of new cloth unto an old garment, for that which is put in to fill it up taketh from the garment, and the rent is made worse. Neither do men put new wine into old bottles: else the bottles break, and the wine runneth out, and the bottles perish: but they put new wine into new bottles, and both are preserved.

Matthew 9: 16–17

And I will pray the Father, and he shall give you another Comforter, that he may abide with you for ever.

John 14: 16

The Lord was really good. I remember on one occasion, I received an email from Sister Debra informing me that some UNICTR Christian Fellowship members had contributed some money and that this had been sent to my account without my prior knowledge. I was speechless. My sister-in-law, Josephine, also sent us some money. I gave glory to God and sincerely thanked all of them.

I had contacted Dr. Koirala, the UN medical doctor in the UN mission in Israel to inform him of the situation I was in, and he drove from Jerusalem to Haifa to come and see us at the hospital. I put Dr. Koirala in touch with the UNICTR management. He reviewed the situation, spoke with the neurosurgeons at Rambam Hospital, and reported back to the chief of administration and the registrar of

And Moses was an hundred and twenty years old when he died: his eye was not dim, nor his natural force abated.

Deuteronomy 34:7

Behold, the Lord's hand is not shortened, that it cannot save; neither his ear heavy, that it cannot hear.

Isaiah 59:1

For the mountains shall depart, and the hills be removed; but my kindness shall not depart from thee, neither shall the covenant of my peace be removed, saith the Lord that hath mercy on thee. O thou afflicted, tossed with tempest, and not comforted, behold, I will lay thy stones with fair colours, and lay thy foundations with sapphires. And I will make thy windows of agates, and thy gates of carbuncles, and all thy borders of pleasant stones. And all thy children shall be taught of the Lord; and great shall be the peace of thy children. In righteousness shalt thou be established: thou shalt be far from oppression; for thou shalt not fear: and from terror; for it shall not come near thee. Behold, they shall surely gather together, but not by me: whosoever shall gather together against thee shall fall for thy sake."

Isaiah 54:10–15

Praise ye the Lord. O give thanks unto the Lord; for he is good: for his mercy endureth for ever. Who can utter the mighty acts of the Lord? who can shew forth all his praise? Blessed are they that keep judgment, and he that doeth righteousness at all times. Remember me, O

That same day, while we were still visiting my husband, one of the nurses came to tell me that there was someone outside looking for me. I walked out of the ICU into the corridor. There I saw a young lady with a paper in her hand. She said, "I'm looking for the Mabika family."

I said, "Yes, we are the Mabika family"

"My name is Colleen," she indicated. "I am here because my pastor has sent me to come and see you." She further explained that her pastor had received an email from a fellow pastor in Chicago, who requested him to look for a family named Mabika, whose husband was critically ill in the hospital and that the said family was stranded in Haifa. And she showed me the email with my name in it, I told her, "Thank you very much for coming." I introduced her to my daughters, and we chatted a bit. I tried to find out what was the name of the pastor who had sent her pastor the email. I thanked God for sending people to us.

When we went back to the hotel in the evening, I contacted my sister Jeannine in the United States of America to try to find out who was that pastor in the US who sent the email. My sister said that one of her prayer partner and good friend of the family, Maggy, whom I also knew, had been praying with her over my husband's situation and us. Maggy was the one who contacted the pastor in Chicago to see whether he knew someone in Haifa whom he could request to come and check on us and give her feedback. This was how Colleen came to visit us.

That same evening, during our prayer time, we cancelled the idea of pneumonia and vasospasm, using the Word of God. By that time, many friends and brothers and sisters in Christ had been calling—Bishop Shumbusho and his spouse; my UNICTR colleagues such as Sister Debra, Brother George, Brother Madenga; and my church leaders, Pastor Charles and Judith Akwera, as well as the Kenneth family. They were encouraging us using the Word of God, sending us Bible verses that we often read and quoted during our prayer time, and praying for us. Needless to say, my sisters and other relatives, such as my sister-in-law and my niece, were also calling from France, from the States, and from Congo-Brazzaville. Here are some of the Bible verses:

- We prayed to Jehovah Rapha, the Lord who heals, to bring Pascal back from his deep sleep, give him a quick and miraculous recovery, and restore him fully.
- We asked God to give us favor in our logistics—the change of departure dates on our tickets with the various airlines at no fee, the arrangements with the next hotel we would have to find after December 28, the medical insurance to cover Pascal's total hospitalization cost and medical evacuation to France as well as admission cost at a French hospital, and finances to cover all the expenses related to our extended stay in Israel.
- We prayed for unity among the five of us, for peace and joy, for God to give us understanding of the lessons to be drawn from that whole unexpected and incredible experience.

We went to visit Pascal twice a day on the December 27 and 28, but nothing had changed.

In the morning of the twenty-ninth, we checked out of Dan Carmel Hotel and took a taxi to go downtown to settle in another hotel we had booked, Colony Hotel. By now, most of the hotels had rooms available. Colony Hotel was located in the town center on one of the well-known streets in Haifa, and it was much nearer to the hospital. On the days when there weren't many buses, we would walk to the hospital. That day, when we reached the ICU to visit Pascal, the social welfare lady, who also spoke French and had helped us before with all the administrative papers of the hospital, came to see me in Pascal's ward and informed me that the head doctor of the ICU wanted to see me. She took me to the doctor's office, which was located within the ICU. She said, "Your husband is not waking up. We have signs that your husband might have pneumonia or vasospasm. This could be the reason why he's not waking up." In my mind and spirit, I rebuked that idea in Jesus's name and kept believing that my husband would wake up. She said they would run some tests and inform me later.

I looked around and saw three other patients, all in the same state and plugged to the same type of machines. They also seemed unconscious. On the left side of the ward door, there was a small desk and a computer, where a nurse stationed there was continually monitoring the patients. The ward was well lit and quiet, except for the noise of the machines connected to the patients, which were going up and down, breathing for the patients. It was a gruesome sight.

I looked at Pascal's lifeless body for a short while, prayed for twenty minutes, and went out in order to give my daughters time to come in also and see their father for ten minutes each. The visiting time was for one hour, from 11:00 a.m. to 12:00 p.m. and from 7:00 p.m. to 8:00 pm.

Seeking God's Intervention

Back at the hotel, we informed our relatives, friends, and colleagues abroad that Pascal had not woken up and that we needed their prayers. I told my daughters that their father's condition was critical. We therefore had to take a stand in God and pray as we never did before. I thanked our heavenly father for the daughters he entrusted with us. They were so supportive.

We decided to fast and pray for Pascal and organize a chain prayer from midnight to six in the morning so that one of us would always be praying while the others were resting. My daughters would take turns one hour each, from that time until 4:00 a.m., and I would take from 4:00 a.m. until 6:00 a.m. We started praying and fasting, coupled with a chain prayer. The collective prayer that night was focused on the following:

- We rendered thanks to God for all the Christians sites we had been able to visit and the spiritual lessons we had learned, the successful head operations Pascal had undergone, the favor God had given us with the hotel we were in, and the food we were eating.

A few minutes later, I saw her coming back, followed by Dr. Amsalem. I quickly ran toward him, saying, "Dr. Amsalem, my husband did not wake up!" I thought I was telling him something new. "What happened? You told me that we could see him today."

Dr. Amsalem calmly responded, "I know he did not wake up this morning."

"Oh, you knew?"

"Yes, I was told he did not wake up. But I cannot tell you why he didn't. Normally, he should have awakened. But you never know really. Patients are different, and they respond differently to treatment. Let's give him time to wake up. Come back in the evening, and we will see."

I felt eased by his calm attitude to the situation. He was not as panicked as I was. I thanked him and left after agreeing that we would stay in touch. I joined my daughters in the waiting room and told them I had found Dr. Amsalem and what he had said. We decided to go back to our hotel and come back in the evening.

We were all silent on our way to the bus stop. We rested for a few hours and took buses again to go back to the hospital. Unfortunately, the situation had not changed. My husband did not still wake up. But this time, we were allowed to see him. The military man keeping watch over the ICU let us in one after the other. I went in first. But before I entered the ward where my husband was, I was given a green medical robe to wear and a disinfectant to clean my hands.

When I entered, the sight was terrifying. My eyes fell straight on my husband. He was lying on his back, connected to several drips and medical apparatuses, including one that was making noise as if breathing in his stead. The bottle at the end of the small tube running from his head was full of blood; another bottle was on the floor to recover his urine with a long tube disappearing under his bed cover. Several other tubes from the nose and the mouth were extended and connected to a long monitoring system that was displaying figures of different colors as if to indicate the status of various parts of his body. Pascal's eyes were closed, and his whole body was still.

my daughters to go and wait for me in the waiting room for families while I would go and try to find the surgery unit of Dr. Amsalem.

I left my children and ran along the corridor to the lifts, trying to remember the floors that we had taken the last time I was with the medics. The lifts we had taken were the lifts for medical personnel with patients only. Now that I had to use the normal lifts, I could not remember exactly my way to Dr. Amsalem's surgery room. With anxiety, I spent some time trying to find my way since there were no directions that I could read or understand.

After a while, I got to a door on a level below that I believed was the door to the surgery unit of Dr. Amsalem. I looked at the corridor on my right, and there was no one, then I looked behind at the corridor I had just come from, and there was no one else there, either. I was stuck. I thought, *Lord, how am I going to get in here? I don't have a badge.* While I was staring at the door, all of a sudden, I saw a hand come over my head and place a badge against the swipe-card terminal to open the door. I was startled because I had not heard anyone approaching me. The door slid open. My first reaction was to turn around to see who had opened the door since the person did not talk to me or ask me anything. I saw the back of a man going up the corridor dressed in a doctor's gown. I only had time to shout out, "Thank you, sir!" as I rushed in before the door closed back.

I found myself again in that little space between the two doors, hoping that someone would come out for me to go through the second door. Some five minutes or so later, that door opened and two nurses came out, and I quickly rushed inside before the second door closed behind me. Once I was inside, a lady caught sight of me and quickly came out from a glass cubicle with her eyes opened wide, wondering what I was doing there. She approached me and signaled with her hands that I was not supposed to be there and I should go back outside. I said to her, "Please, Dr. Amsalem! Dr. Amsalem!" trying to explain why I was there. Noticing how distraught I was, she did not insist that I leave and turned back to where she had come from and disappeared.

THE DARK VALLEY WITH A GLIMPSE OF LIGHT

The Coma

After breakfast, we asked information from the hotel reception on how to go to Rambam hospital by bus. For the first time, we ventured outside with no guide and tried to catch the buses to get to the hospital. After waiting for a while at a bus stop, there seemed to be no bus coming. We looked for a taxi that could take the five of us. We reached the hospital just in time for the visiting hours. In front of the door of the ICU, there was a military guard keeping watch, and we found many people waiting there for their turn to enter. When our turn came, we proceeded to enter, but the military man did not let us in and told us to wait. He went inside the intensive care unit and came back shortly after with a female doctor, who I found out later on was the head of the ICU.

The doctor, peeking from the door, asked, "Mabika?" I said yes, and she said, "Oh…your husband did not wake up."

We were shocked. "What? What do you mean he didn't wake up?"

"He did not wake up. Try to come back in the evening and see." She closed the door and disappeared.

My heart started beating very fast. I was completely at a loss, wondering what I was going to do. I remembered that Dr. Amsalem had given me his card to call him in case of need. I took the card from my bag and called him. It rang, but there was no response. I then told had said, "You have not yet started preparing your songs of praise." I understood it was now time to sing those songs of praise. I shared this with my daughters. We praised and worshipped God! Our hearts were full of thanksgiving! In the hotel, the Christmas Eve party was in full swing in one of the halls. We could hear the music from our rooms. When we finished, we exchanged Christmas gifts. I handed over to them the CDs of the Word of God that their father had prepared for each one of them. Then I told my daughters not to unpack the bags as we were to leave the hotel the next morning because the rooms had been given to us just for that night. So we went to bed and soundly slept.

The next morning, we went to the restaurant for breakfast. It was a real feast. The restaurant was really spacious, with different types of breakfast. My daughters and I chose a table, and we went to help ourselves as it was self-service. While we were eating, we saw a waiter coming toward us with a note on a tray. He said, "This is for you." I was a bit surprised, wondering what the note was, as I knew we were to check out after breakfast. When I read the note, it said, "Mrs. Mabika, you may stay in the hotel with your children until Tuesday, twenty-eight of December." It was such a relief. My daughters and I thanked God for his provision.

When we finished breakfast, we went back to our rooms to unpack and rest. That same day after breakfast, Isaac came to take us to visit Jerusalem, the Wailing Wall, and the Dolorosa Church. When we came back, I told Isaac that we had decided to discontinue the guided tour and stay in Haifa, close to Pascal. We profusely thanked him and gave him a small souvenir from Arusha that we had brought and promised to keep in touch with him. My daughters and I spent the night and woke up the next morning, December 26, a Sunday, to see Pascal.

building, Danny came out of his car and someone got in and drove his car away. We got out of our minivan and the hotel valets quickly went to the boot to get our luggage.

When we entered the reception hall of the hotel, I looked at Danny in amazement, wondering where he was taking us. At the reception desk, Danny said something to the ladies behind the desk, and one of them looked at me and said, "Welcome Mrs. Mabika. Here are the electronic cards to your rooms for tonight, one next to the other on the fourth floor. You must be tired. Go straight up, and the valet will bring your luggage." My children and I were lost for words.

On the way to the lift, I asked Danny, "How did you get this place?" He said, "I called them, but they said they had no rooms. I insisted that they find something, anything, making them understand that it would be a shame for our nation to let you down in your situation as tourists in a state of emergency, especially since you're a woman with daughters and a husband in a critical condition in the hospital. This is why they told me to come and bring you here."

When we got to the rooms and opened them, we had no words. These were very posh rooms. There was one large room with a double bed and a small bed, which Maud, Cap, and I occupied, and the other was an attendant room with two beds, where Eunice and Diyenat stayed. The bathroom had a Jacuzzi and large mirrors. Danny made sure we were well settled in Dan Carmel Hotel. When we accompanied him back down to the reception hall, we sat down and discussed again with him and Charity for a while before he decided to drive back to Tel Aviv that same night or early morning, as it was coming to 1:00 a.m. In our rooms, the children and I thanked God for his ways and provision. From people who were in the street for a whole day and without a place to sleep, all of a sudden, we found ourselves in a mansion on a twenty-fourth of December! We were grateful. In turns, we quickly went to have a shower as we were all exhausted.

We all gathered in one room to give thanks to God. It is then that the Lord reminded me of the dream I had two nights before where he people playing musical instruments here and there. I tried to relax while hoping to get positive news from Danny. He rang me again and indicated that the situation seemed difficult but quickly added that he was going to drive straight away from Tel Aviv to join us so that together we could see what to do. I thanked him for that sacrifice he was making, surprised by that spontaneous offer, knowing that Haifa was about an hour and half or two hours drive from Tel Aviv. He indicated to Isaac a specific place where he was to take us to wait for him.

Night had fallen. The city of Haifa was lit with colorful lights. Most of the public places were full, especially restaurants or coffee places. We went to one coffee place and ordered some ice creams while waiting for Danny. I was still thinking, *Lord, there is no way I am going to be stranded with children, with no place to sleep, on a twenty-fourth of December, with my husband in a hospital critically ill.* The similarity with the situation of Mary, Joseph, and Baby Jesus came to my mind. I smiled. My daughters and I forgot our situation for a while. We were looking at and commenting on what was going on around us, the people, the music, the decorations.

Time went by. By the time Danny arrived, it was after 11:00 p.m. He came with Charity. He introduced himself. This was the first time we were meeting him and seeing him face to face, although I had spoken to him on several occasions for the arrangements of the trip. He sat down and chatted with us for a while, reassuring us that he would do his best to find us something. I thanked him again for leaving his family and driving all the way just to come and assist us on a Christmas Eve. There again, I saw the hand of God showing us that he was with us. After half an hour or so, Danny's mobile rang, so he went outside to pick the call. When he came back, he told us to get back into our car with our driver and follow them.

We drove behind them for a while; it seemed away from the city center. His car was driving along various streets that were going up and down, leading toward a hill to a well-lit huge building—a hotel on top of the hill. When both cars stopped in front of the porch of the he could have easily given that task to any other assistant. The Lord was really watching over my children and me in that distress.

In the City of Haifa

Isaac, our children and I left the hospital to go and look for a hotel. We went to the hotels that Isaac knew. There was no room available. On 24th December 2010, in the afternoon, the city center of Haifa was busy and had colorful decorations along the main streets. We continued to drive around, still in search for hotels, but in vain. We stopped at one restaurant along the main street to have a bite. We were feeling tired.

While the children were reviewing the menu, I was thinking, *Lord, where am I going to stay with my daughters?* In the context of our organized and guided tour, there was no provision for a visit in Haifa. We seemed lost. Then an idea came to my mind—call the manager of Vered H. Tour and explain to him our predicament. His name was Danny. I looked for his number on the hotel bookings we had and found it. I went out of the restaurant and called him. I indicated to him that while I was in the hospital, my daughters had slept in one hotel and that it was just for that one night and that now we had gone around and had found no rooms available in all the hotels we had been to with the driver and if he could help us secure a hotel accommodation. He said he was in Tel Aviv and that he would call me back after making a few calls.

I went back inside the restaurant. By this time, food had been served and the children and Isaac had started eating. I reported to them what Danny had said. About forty-five minutes later, Danny called me back. His response was not very encouraging. He said he had made a few calls to people he knew and had not been successful. It was a high season in Haifa and all the hotels seemed fully booked. He said he would continue to do his best and would call me again. We finished eating and came out of the restaurant and got into our car.

The main street where we were was now full of people. The festive atmosphere of the Christmas Eve was settling in. There was music,

After this briefing, Dr. Amsalem told me to follow him to the medical staff room, where he was planning to make calls to help us find a hotel. He told me to sit in one of the armchairs and started making calls. He consulted a couple of his colleagues in the room in Hebrew. I guessed he was asking them if they knew any hotel that might not be fully booked, as they all seemed to be. From time to time, his work mobile would ring and he would answer and carry on looking for a hotel. Some fifteen minutes later, he told me, "All the hotels in Haifa seemed to be booked. I've contacted a convent to explain the situation as they usually have spare rooms for emergency cases. But the head nun was not there so I left my number for her to call me back. I suggest that you go to the hotels yourself with your daughters and inquire for rooms." I thanked him, and we walked out of the staff room.

As we were walking along the corridor, many people were greeting the doctor. He then went his way, and I went to pick my daughters from the meeting room where I had left them. When we were coming back through the corridor next to the intensive care unit, one of the nurses who had seen us a couple of times with Dr. Amsalem said to us kindly, "Do you know who you were speaking with?"

I naturally replied, "Yes, he's the doctor who just operated on my husband."

She continued, "Do you know who he is? He is the top neurosurgeon here in Israel. In fact, you are lucky to have had him to operate on your husband. I heard he was supposed to be on leave today. He came in this morning to the hospital to check a few things before taking off, and then he was presented the file of your husband for instructions on what to do. He decided to stay and take care of your husband's case himself."

When I heard this, I could not believe my ears. My first reaction was to thank God. I realized then how much this doctor had done for my children and me. He had taken time, despite the many calls he was receiving on his mobile, to explain to us the details of the medical condition of my husband and assist us in identifying a hotel with free rooms in the afternoon of the twenty-fourth of December 2010 when

Back to Intensive Care Unit

A few minutes later, I saw the medics pushing my husband on the bed. This time, the sight of him was even worse than the first time. He seemed to have even more tubes and drips than the previous operation, and his eyes were completely shut with tubes coming out of his nose and mouth. I followed the medics up to the Intensive Care Unit. The medics went inside while I stayed outside as I was not allowed to go in. After installing him there, they came out and left.

While I was moving toward my small resting room, I saw my family come in with our driver Isaac in the corridor. I greeted them and asked them how they spent the night and I thanked Isaac for taking care of them. At that moment, I thanked God for Isaac because he had not left us for a single minute since the whole thing started. He had been taking care of my daughters and me as if we were his family. My daughters told me that the hotel they had slept in was only for that night—it was called Colony Hotel—and that we had to go and look for another one together. I indicated to them that the doctor who had operated on their father, Dr. Amsalem, would come and see us in the next few minutes. So we should wait before going out since we were not allowed to see their dad until December 26. I also told them that God had been good since Dr. Amsalem spoke French, and they were also pleasantly surprised.

Dr. Amsalem came, and I introduced my daughters and Isaac to him. He told us to follow him along the corridor to one of the meeting rooms. In the room, there was a large conference table with chairs and a projector. He started telling my daughters what had happened to my husband in medical terms and what he had done during his surgery. My daughters seized that opportunity to ask him a lot of questions—how did their father get the aneurism, do they have it themselves, and how could they make sure that they didn't have it. Dr. Amsalem reassured them that aneurysm is congenital. He explained to them the same things he had told me before the surgery.

how my husband was doing after the second surgery. I thanked her, and we hung up.

Then I contacted our relatives in Congo-Brazzaville, in France, and in the USA. I also called my church to inform my pastor, Charles Akwera, and his spouse, Judith Akwera, of the situation and requested their prayers. Later, I phoned the Kenneth family, Bishop John Shumbusho, and our ICTR fellowship members, as well as the Mutigas in Nairobi. I hung around until the two hours elapsed. Afterward, I headed back to the surgery room to meet Dr. Amsalem. Standing in front of the door of the surgery room, I had to wait until someone came out for me to enter since I did not have a badge to get in. I moved into the small space between the two doors and waited on the two-person bench. I started looking anxiously at my watch, counting the minutes since the two hours had gone by.

Twenty minutes later, Dr. Amsalem came out of the surgery room. I looked at him, my heart beating fast. He said in French "The operation went well. You will see him pass by with the medics. They will take him for a head scan, and afterward, you can go with them to accompany him to the intensive care unit. You will not be able to see him for the next two days because we've given him medicine to sleep continuously for forty-eight hours as we've touched his brain a great deal. So it is only on December 26 that you will be able to see him, around lunchtime. You can go back to your hotel and give me a call if there is anything."

This is when I told him "I do not have a hotel to go to because I've been sleeping in the hospital since I arrived with my husband. I don't even know where my daughters are as we speak. They must be looking for me. I hope they will come and look for me where they left me last night."

Dr. Amsalem wondered "Oh, you don't have a hotel? Let me finish with a few things, and I will find you at the ICU in the next half hour." I thanked him, and he departed.

back to me with the charger. I asked her how much I could pay for the charger, and she indicated with her hands that I could leave with it and without having to pay. I insisted on giving her a little token of gratitude. Then I left the shop and went somewhere less busy where I could make the calls.

I wasn't sure that the roaming was going to work. My first call was to Mr. Adama Dieng, registrar of the International Criminal Tribunal for Rwanda, our employer. He was the assistant secretary general and head of the mission. So I dialed his number I had on my phone; it rang, and he picked the call. By this time, it was around noon. I told him that I was in a difficult situation, as my husband was being operated on in a hospital following a brain hemorrhage while we were on a few days' vacation with the family. He was shocked. He asked, "Which country are you in?" I answered, "Israel." Then he indicated that he was going to immediately contact the UN medical officer who was also away from the duty station on leave. He was very sympathetic and asked me to keep him posted on the developments of the situation.

Then I called the chief of administration, Ms. Sarah Kilemi. When the phone rang, she was also on leave with her family somewhere in Asia. When I broke the news to her, she was in disbelief. She could not believe her ears. I told her I was alone with my four daughters and that I was expecting Pascal to come out of the surgery ward. She also informed me that she was going to contact the people at the UN clinic in Arusha to get in touch with me.

As soon as I hung up with her, my phone rang. Startled, I answered. I was happy to hear the voice of the UNICTR medical doctor, Dr. Epee Fernandez. She said the registrar had given her the news and she was calling back to find out what exactly happened. I related the whole story to her. She said, "Fortunately, you were in Israel when something like that happens, where they have all medical facilities, because had it happened in Arusha, well, I don't know what we would have done." She indicated that she would call me back after a few hours to find out

At the Basement of the Hospital

By this time, I realized that my mobile phone from Tanzania was dead and I did not have my charger with me. The local SIM card that we had bought was with my daughters. I had not heard from them since they left with Isaac. I wanted this time to call my office to inform them of what was going on? what was going on with my family. I had no means of contact. So I started going around the few shops that were in the basement to see if I could buy a charger. There was an electronic shop where I hoped to find a charger. I went there, but there was no charger that could fit on my mobile phone. So I left and continued going around in circles looking for a charger. I passed a mini supermarket that even had a pharmacy desk, but there was nothing.

Then I saw a shop selling toys for children. I was walking past the display window when I saw a lady who was keeping the shop standing behind a counter. When I met her eyes, she smiled and beckoned me to come into the shop. Knowing that it was a shop for children's toys, I shook my head to indicate that I was not going there. I lifted the phone in my hand, pointing at it to show her what I was looking for. But the lady kept beckoning me in. So finally I went in.

I tried to explain to her using gestures that I was looking for a charger for my phone. She took the phone from my hands and examined it. She then put the phone on the counter and went through a door that was at the back of the store. She came out with two chargers. She tried the first one, and it did not fit. But the second one was the right charger. I was so relieved, and I thanked God for this unexpected blessing. The lady then took my phone and plugged it in a socket next to her in the shop. I very much thanked her and explained that I would come back later.

Now that my mind was a little bit at peace, I decided to go and have some tea. I went to take a seat in the middle of the court, where there were many tables and chairs. While I was having my tea, I was thinking about all the people I had to contact as soon as possible. Half an hour later, I went to pick up the phone. The lady handed it over

I was speechless again. He went on to explain that an aneurism is like a pimple, which suddenly appears on your face without you knowing and when it is fully grown, it bursts. Then I asked, "How come this was not seen or brought to attention despite all the medical checkups he has had in his life?"

Dr. Amsalem responded, "It is not an ailment or a sickness that you can go ask a doctor to check for. Even I as a medical doctor cannot go ask another doctor to check for an aneurism in my head. It will not be seen. We only know a person has had an aneurism when it has burst." Then he went on to explain further using the second screen and showed me a vein on my husband's head that had a small bump on it. He pointed at that bump on the vein. "This is what burst and created the hemorrhage. My job now, which is a very delicate one, will consist in stitching the place where the vein burst to prevent further hemorrhage, making sure not to block the vein or cut it. By the way Mrs. Mabika, I saw your husband has a French passport, but I was told he came from Tanzania."

I told him, "Indeed, we are French nationals working for the UN in Arusha, Tanzania." The doctor then said something interesting, that he had lived in France for a year while on training. I was so excited to meet an Israeli who could understand and speak French. I asked, "So we can continue speaking in French then?" He answered yes. From then on, our conversations were in French.

After he had explained everything I needed to know, he said, "You look tired. Go to the basement of the hospital. There are some shops and cafeterias where you can have something to drink and come back and meet me in two hours' time at the place where I saw you the first time."

"Thank you, Doctor." Before we parted, I asked anxiously, "Is it going to be okay?"

He answered honestly and cautiously, "You know how to pray? Well, pray for me." He then left and went back to the surgery unit. I followed down the corridor up to the lift and went down to the basement of the hospital, where I was surprised to find small shops and a food court.

The doctor turned his head to see who was there, catching a glimpse of me before the door closed. I sat back on the bench between the two closed doors.

Immediately, the second door opened again and here came the doctor who had seen me. He was tall and young looking. I stood up, as I knew he came to speak to me. He shook my hand and introduced himself as Dr. Amsalem and said, "I am the one who is going to operate on your husband. I have five minutes, and I like to explain to you what I'm going to do. Please follow me."

He opened the first door with his badge, and we turned left into the other corridor. He stopped in front of one door and opened it. That room was cold and completely dark. He put the light on, and I saw many computer screens lined up. He sat behind one desk that had a keyboard laid on it. He typed in "Pascal Mabika" as he said it aloud. All the screens suddenly came on. I was taken aback as I saw my husband's name written out on top of the screens with images of his skull and all the veins in his head showing. The first screen on my left-hand side was totally dark. Then Dr. Amsalem started explaining to me.

"The black screen that you see here does not mean that it is not working. It works. But this is how your husband was brought in last night. His brain was totally covered with blood. That's why you cannot see anything. Let us move to the second screen."

I was listening attentively, saying nothing at this time.

"This screen, which is now clear, with the skull of your husband visible, reflects the operation that he just underwent this morning. It consisted in removing the blood that had covered his brain."

At this stage, I asked him anxiously, "What caused the hemorrhage? My husband was not sick…"

"Your husband had an aneurism."

The lost look in my face indicated to him that I needed further explanation. I asked, "How did he get it?"

"He did not get it from anywhere. He was born with it."

in Hebrew. As soon as they reached us, one of them spoke to me in English, "How can I help you, Madam?" So I explained my situation, indicating that my husband had just been operated downstairs from the head and that another operation was due to take place right away in another surgery unit but I did not know exactly where. This is when he said, "It must be at the neurosurgery unit." He tried to explain to me where it was, but I begged his indulgence to accompany me there as I had been looking for the place for a while but to no avail. I was grateful the man showed me the way to the place, again in the underground.

The door of the neurosurgery unit was at an intersection of two corridors, one on the right-hand side and the one we had just walked down. He opened the door with his badge to let me in and left. As soon as I entered the room through the sliding door, the door immediately closed behind me, and unfortunately, right in front of me was another sliding door that I could not open. So I found myself in between two closed doors in a very tiny space where I could see a bench made for two people to sit. So I decided to sit down, wondering whether I was in the right place. Thank God, the door behind me slid open and I saw the same tall medics bringing my husband in.

I was so happy I could see my husband for a few minutes. By this time, I could not recognize his face. He had a huge tube in his mouth with plasters around to hold it. There were two thinner tubes going through his nostrils and another tube coming from his head down to a half-full huge bottle of blood. My husband's head, which was always shaved, was covered with a large plaster that held the tube coming out of his head. He was unconscious. I was lost for words.

The medics opened the second door with their badges and went in with my husband. I knew I could not follow them in, and the door immediately closed behind them. I stood in this small space in between two walls, wondering what was going to happen next. After about five minutes, that second door opened and two nurses came through. Just before the door closed behind them, I quickly peeped in and saw a medical doctor with his back to me, writing something on a notepad.

waiting area. I waited peacefully. Forty-five minutes later, the swinging doors opened again. A doctor came out and walked toward us in the waiting area. I saw him passing the other people and walking toward me. I automatically stood up. I was trying anxiously to read the look in his eyes, wondering if it was going to be good news or bad news. My heart was pounding in my chest.

The doctor came close to me and said, "The operation went well. In the next few minutes, he's going to be taken to another surgery unit…" He continued speaking, but in fact, I did not catch again what he said because my mind stopped at "another surgery unit." I inquired, "Surgery unit? Another operation? How many operations are there going to be?" He did not answer my questions, but I heard him continue talking. "Do not wait for your husband here. Go quickly to…unit… with Doctor…and wait for him there." I did not catch everything he said as my mind was still in shock of the news of the second immediate operation. I was thinking about all the waiting I had just done and then I would not be able to see him. Then the doctor left. When I gathered my mind, I tried to remember the name of the doctor and the surgery unit he had just mentioned.

It was now around 10:45 a.m. on December 24, 2010. In the hospital, all indications were written in Hebrew, Arabic, or Russian. It was difficult for me to find my way. I walked to a lift, went up, and came out on the first floor. I asked a nurse I met where I could find the neurosurgery. But unfortunately, she could not give me much information because she did not speak English. I went back into the lift and went up another level to the second floor. I came out onto a hall where a man was standing behind a desk. I was happy to see someone who looked like a receptionist and walked quickly toward him. I inquired from him where was the neurosurgery unit. Here also, we did not seem to understand each other. I tried to indicate to him that I was looking for a place for operations on the head gesturing with my hands.

Fortunately, right at that time, two medics were passing by. The man behind the desk called them and explained something to them

In the Surgery Rooms

The waiting area was an intersection of two corridors. There were six or seven people waiting, and no one looked foreign. I sat down, but I quickly got up again. My mind was boiling. I had not yet told any family member back home or from my office about the situation. There was a long corridor on the left side of the waiting room. I started pacing up and down the corridor, praying in tongues, speaking to Jehovah Rapha, the Healer. Time seemed long.

An hour later, the swinging doors opened. One doctor came out. I stood still in anticipation that he would come and speak to me. But he walked toward another group of people. So I turned back, continuing to pace up and down. I just could not sit down. This time, I was coming from the end of the corridor back toward the waiting room. I saw someone from the other end walking up the corridor. This man walked past everybody in the waiting area and continued toward me. I continued walking down, sticking to my side of the corridor.

At one point, the man suddenly turned toward my side of the corridor and stood right in front of me. I stopped short surprised. All of a sudden, the man started speaking to me in English as if he knew I did not speak Hebrew, Russian, or Arabic. He said, "I want you to know that you are in good hands. You see me standing before you. I could not sit…I could not move…I could not talk. I was in bed for three months. But these people"—his hand pointed toward the surgery block—"are the ones who operated me. Now I can walk and talk. The doctors here are very good. I want you to trust them." He then walked off without giving me time to realize what he had just told me.

After processing what I had just heard, I turned around to see if I could catch up with him and talk. But he was gone. I stood in amazement of what had just happened, wondering why this man had spoken only to me and to no one else in the waiting area. I felt peace in my heart. In my spirit, I had the conviction that God had spoken to me to calm me down. So for the first time, I went and took a seat in the hemorrhage. Please be strong and pray. I will be there with you, and I will be praying for you." And he nodded back. The medics understood that I was a family member. So I followed them.

We entered a lift, went down to a certain floor, and then we followed a long corridor. There was no one. It looked as if we were underground. At the end of the corridor, they pushed wide open a double door, and the door closed behind us when we passed through. We entered another empty corridor with clean white walls all along. The walls did not reach the ceiling, and the top part was made of glass. From the glass, I could see lights that reminded me of operation theatres.

When we reached the end of the corridor, we turned left into what seemed to be a waiting room. Immediately after, two doctors came in to meet us. One of them spoke to me, asking, "What happened?"

I told him, "We had been vacationing in Tiberias as a family. Following a dip in the Jordan River, my husband all of a sudden felt unwell and fainted. He was quickly taken to Poriya Medical Center, where they diagnosed a brain hemorrhage. Yesterday, he was brought in on transfer, and this is why he is here."

The doctor listened and said, "I see. Does he take any medicine?" I said yes and showed him the medicine my husband takes regularly for his blood pressure. The doctor asked, "Is this all he takes?" and again I responded yes. He looked at the medicine and said, "I know it," and he kept it in his hands. Then he told me that I was going to be accompanied back out to the waiting room. He addressed the medics in Hebrew, and one of them walked back with me while the others went away with my husband and the doctor.

My heart was broken as I saw my husband being taken away. I stood there sobbing. All sorts of thoughts came into my mind. I was wondering whether I was going to see my husband again. Then the medic took me by the arm to escort me to the waiting area where all family members wait for their relatives to come out of surgery.

six forty-five in the morning. So I stood in front of that door waiting for the doctors to come out.

After a time that seemed very long, the door opened. Many doctors came out of the room. The first people were surprised to see me right in front of the door as I believed they weren't expecting to see anyone at that time. Their eyes widened in surprise. As they came out one after the other, I wondered who I was supposed to speak to. Then one of them was still getting out of the doctor's room and saw me. He walked directly toward me. I believe, as I was black, he assumed that I was a relative of the gentleman who had been brought in the night before and whom they had been talking about.

He said, "Mabika?"

I responded, "Yes, I am Mrs. Mabika."

He said, "I am happy to see you. But I do not have much time to talk to you. It is seven forty-five now. At eight o'clock, your husband has to be taken to the surgery room. I want you to know that his life is in danger. If you know how to pray, you may pray for him. I am going to make preparations, but you can go back to the ICU and wait at the door. Some medics will come and take your husband, and you'll be able to see him and accompany him to the surgery unit." I said, "Thank you, Doctor!" and he immediately walked away.

So I did as he said. I walked back to the door of the ICU and waited. A few minutes later, from the other end of the corridor, I saw two medics coming toward the ICU, pushing a bed. I was impressed by their height and build. They reached the ICU, opened the door, and walked in, while I waited outside, as I was not allowed to enter. A few minutes later, they came out with my husband on the bed. I quickly held my husband's hand, trying to see how he was doing. He seemed to be sleeping. When I shook his hand to wake him up, he startled and mumbled a few words.

Calling him by his nickname, I said, "Pabi, Pabi, it's me!" I held his hand firmly as he was being pulled away by the medics. "They're taking you to the surgery room for an operation. They said you have a brain

GOD WITH ME

Move to the Surgery Rooms

Early morning came. Around 6:00 a.m., I got up, put the waiting room in order, and went to the ladies' room to have a quick wash, while the cleaners started cleaning the corridors of the unit and the nurses were moving up and down, taking care of patients in the various wards. I followed the corridor up to the door of the intensive-care ward, where they had taken my husband into. The door was tightly closed. One of the nurses told me that it was too early for any visitor and that the visiting hours were from 11:00 a.m. to 12:00 p.m. and from 7:00 p.m. to 8:00 p.m. I explained to her that I wanted to see my husband who was brought in just the night before. She advised that I wait for the doctor, who would be arriving by 7:00 a.m., in one of the rooms at the other end of the corridor. I thanked her and moved away toward the other end of the corridor.

As I started pacing up and down the corridor, waiting for the time to see the doctor, I passed by many closed doors, and it was difficult to know which one was an office or which one was a ward. I was trying to locate the door of the doctor's office. While I was slowly walking along the corridor, I overheard voices from one of the closed doors. I heard voices speaking Hebrew, which I did not understand, but in the midst of the flow of words, I heard the mention of "Pascal Mabika," my husband's name. I stopped short in front of that door and waited. I said to myself, *They are talking about my husband. What are they saying?* Then I said, *Lord, whatever it is, please give them wisdom.* It was around

My mind was boiling. I had no sleep. I paced up and down praying. I did not have the courage to call anyone abroad to inform them of the news. I continued to pray. At 2:00 a.m I walked out to see the nurse on night duty at the reception in the corridor leading to the ICU. I wanted to inquire how my husband was doing at that time. She picked the phone receiver at the reception and called the nurse inside the ICU. A few minutes later, she said that my husband was sleeping. I went back to my waiting room to continue to pray. After a while, I lay down on the sofa trying to get some sleep. Nothing. I kept looking at the ceiling in the dim light until I dozed off.

I rushed quickly back to where I had left Pascal. I found the new scan of his head was done. This other doctor in the waiting ward informed me that they had checked his brain again and confirmed the hemorrhage and that Pascal was to be taken to the intensive-care unit for the night in another building within the hospital premises. I informed my children and Isaac, and we all followed the medics who were pushing my husband's bed to the ICU.

In the Intensive Care Unit

Just before the medics took Pascal inside the ICU, they stopped at the door and addressed him by asking him a few questions, such as "How are you?" "Okay!" he responded. "Where are you now?" "I am on a sickbed… I guess," he answered. Then the medics looked at me and nodded in an attempt to tell me that Pascal was still conscious. Then Pascal was taken inside, but I could not enter as the ICU was out of bounds at that time of the night. The medics came out and left.

We were still standing at the closed door of the ICU when a doctor on a night duty came and told us that Pascal was to spend the night there and that we could go back home. It was then that I explained the situation to him, specifying that we had no home nor hotel, that we were tourists who just arrived from Tiberias and that we did not know where we were to spend the night. I told him that my children and Isaac were to go away to look for a hotel accommodation, but I insisted to stay there to spend the night in the hospital to be close to my husband. He indicated that they had no beds for family members and that I really had to go. I told him that I was ready to sleep anywhere, even on a chair or in an office, as long as I stayed near my husband. He guided me to a sort of waiting room where there were some two-seater sofas and gave me a blanket and a pillow. I was thankful. There was nobody inside, considering the late time in the night. I laid my bed, switched of the light, and sat down in the dim light.

between the buildings we left in Tiberias, those I was seeing past as the ambulance was racing forward and those that I saw in Haifa.

Immediately, two medics appeared and opened the back of the ambulance to take the stretcher on which Pascal was. I jumped out of the ambulance and followed the two medics and the doctor inside the hospital. My children and Isaac were told to remain in the lobby. Pascal was put on a bed and placed in a corner in a place that appeared to be a waiting ward while the doctor was talking to another doctor, explaining to him the situation. I went and stood next to my husband, doing my best to comfort him. He was agitated. At one point, he requested to be taken to the men's room. When he returned, the doctor told me that he was going to take him for another scan and that in the meantime I should go the reception to fill in the admission paper and contact my husband's medical insurance and inform them accordingly.

On my way to the reception, I met my children and Isaac and told them what I was about to do. As a family, our UN medical insurance was Vanbreda International located in Belgium. I suddenly remembered that we did not travel with our medical-insurance cards. Fortunately, our daughter Eunice had hers on her in her wallet. So I quickly used my Tanzanian mobile phone (thank God it was roaming!) to try to make the call to Belgium. It was already 9:00 p.m. on December 23, and I was not sure I was going to get anyone on the line.

I was so thankful when someone picked my call. I explained to the man on the line that we were on vacation in Israel as a family, that my husband had been admitted in Rambam Hospital in Haifa for a brain hemorrhage, and that the hospital needed a guarantee letter for his treatment. The man was so helpful. He asked me for the fax number of the hospital. The receptionist gave it to me. In the next ten minutes, the letter came in.

I thanked God for having taken care of that issue. At the reception, the doctor who had accompanied my husband from Poriya Medical Center showed me a paper to sign for my husband's transfer to Rambam Hospital and then bid us farewell as he returned to Tiberias. Afterward,

THE LONG NIGHT

Transfer to Rambam Medical Center in Haifa

The ambulance was waiting outside. My husband was placed at the back with the accompanying doctor. Inside, there was life-saving medical equipment, such as oxygen bottles. As I took a seat in front with the driver, I was saying to myself, *Father, I am sure one day you will tell us why all this is happening*. My children and Isaac were following the ambulance. And off we went!

My mind was boiling. I was trying to think and figure out what had just occurred. I wanted to pray, but I couldn't. I just did not know what to tell God. I spontaneously started to pray in tongues. The prayer came out of my mouth so smoothly like water. All the way through, I prayed in tongues as I have never done before. The ambulance, with a siren sound and the revolving light, was racing past many cars, and at traffic lights, it was being given right of way. While it was speeding off, I would from time to time look back to try to see how my husband was behaving. I would see the doctor very busy giving him oxygen or checking his pulse. My husband appeared restless.

My heart was pounding in my chest. I was not crying. I was not thinking about anything else but God, for him to do something quickly so that my husband could recover. As I was in that spirit and prayer, in no time, the ambulance drove into the compound of Rambam Medical Center, maybe after one hour and thirty minutes. I had not realized we had entered the city of Haifa, as I could not see the difference

An hour or so later, my husband was brought back. The doctor came out and told me, "Your husband has a brain hemorrhage. This hospital is not equipped for this type of ailment. I have made arrangements for him to be transferred to the biggest hospital, which is in Haifa. I have already contacted and informed them. The ambulance is ready. I am coming with you." As you can imagine, this news came as a shock to me. I looked at him, my body trembling. I was speechless. Haifa was about two hours' drive from Poriya Medical Center.

One came, speaking English. He asked me what happened. I related to him the incident at the Jordan River. Pascal was still vomiting and complaining of headache. He checked Pascal and decided to put him on drips to stop the vomiting and the headache. He put him on one of the emergency beds, next to the many other patients being treated, and it was separated by a movable partition.

When Pascal was taken care of, I went outside to try to find out any UN staff member in a foreign country whom I could contact in case of emergency. Thank God, Pascal and I, as UN staff members, had our security clearances as required by the United Nations before undertaking any trip outside the duty station. On the clearance, there were phone numbers of many officials, including the UN security coordinator in the country we were to call in case of need. I looked at the time on my watch. It was past 6:30 p.m. on a Thursday, December 23, 2010. I was not sure to find anyone on the line, it being Christmas time and after working hours. Fortunately, I got a man on the line on one of the contact numbers. I explained the situation to him. He gave me the phone number of the UN Mission in Jerusalem where I could get in touch with the UN medical officer. I decided to call the mission in the morning the next day, Friday.

I went back into Pascal's makeshift room. Our daughters were sitting in a waiting area at the entrance and were occasionally popping in to see their father. Nothing had changed. From time to time, Pascal would vomit and complain of headache. In fact, he wanted my hands constantly over his head. This seemed to give him some relief. Anytime I would try to remove them to attend to something else, he would express his disapproval by groaning. Two hours later, no real progress was recorded. The pain would quiet down and come back unabated. About 7:00 p.m, I spoke with the doctor to find out what he was planning to do. He said he would request for a scan of his head. Two medical personnel came with a stretcher and took my husband away. My daughters and I waited. The time seemed long.

my mind, I was saying, *We have just rededicated our lives to the Lord. What could be the problem?* The whole thing just seemed unbelievable, especially since my husband had not been sick nor complained of any discomfort or pain while in Israel. I was praying in tongues while I was holding my husband's head on my lap. None of us was crying. But we had a lot of anguish in our hearts.

Two paramedics came with a stretcher, which they assembled like a chair to enable my husband to sit properly while they were climbing the staircase from the pool to the ambulance waiting in the public area next to the building. Just before they put my husband in the ambulance, he indicated to them that he wanted first to go to the restroom for a pee. To our amazement, I saw my husband getting himself out of the chair/stretcher and walking to the water closets alone without any support. He had apparently said he did not need any. Then I said to myself, *Thank God, his state is not as serious as I feared!* I felt a sense of relief. I seized that opportunity to run quickly to the changing rooms to remove the wet white robe I had and told my daughters to do the same.

When he came back, the paramedics made him lie down on the chair they had retransformed into a stretcher and put in in the ambulance. One of them told me to sit in the front with the driver while they sat at the back with my husband, attending to him. Our daughters went into our car with Isaac. They followed the ambulance. The ambulance drove to the nearest hospital that we reached after a few minutes. It was the Poriya Medical Center in Tiberias.

At Poriya Medical Center

Upon arrival, the two paramedics took my husband out of the ambulance into the emergency unit where we found many other patients and their relatives. The place was packed. It was around 5:30 p.m. Most people there seemed to be speaking Hebrew, Russian, or Arabic languages that my family and I could not understand nor speak. I inquired whether I could have a doctor who understood and spoke French or English.

While I was talking to Capucine, who had just emerged from water, I saw Pascal walking out of the water to go, in my mind, fetch Diyenat, who was waiting for her turn on the steps around the pool while speaking to her sisters Eunice and Maud, who were taking pictures and filming the whole event. All of a sudden, Capucine, still in the river, said loudly, "Daddy has fallen! Look, Mommy! Daddy has fallen behind you!" I looked back and saw my husband sitting flat on the floor, with his legs stretched in front of him. He was holding onto one of the iron bars of the rail designed to help people get into and out of the water. His head was not on the floor.

I quickly ran to him, surprised, calling, "!Pabi!"—the sweet name I call him, a combination of the first two characters of his first name and of my maiden name—"are you all right? What is the problem? What happened?" He did not answer me. It seemed he could not talk. Funny thing, his eyes were fixed, just staring at something in the sky, and I did not know what. I looked in the same direction and saw nothing. I shook him a little bit to see if I could get an answer to my questions.

By this time, many people had gathered around us, including our daughters. We tried to put him back unto his feet but in vain. Very unexpectedly, my husband started vomiting. He vomited and vomited. Then he fainted. Someone in the crowd around said he was a medical doctor and wanted to help. He touched his pulse and checked the other parts of his body, particularly his eyes, asking me a lot of questions, about things such as the last food he had eaten or whether he had been sick. I answered him with everything I knew.

A few minutes later, my husband opened his eyes and faintly said, "I have a headache!" I could see from his face that he was in pain. My heart was racing in my chest. I was wondering what was happening. My husband had been in good health, apart from the medicine he was taking daily for his blood pressure. By this time, an ambulance had arrived, called by someone I did not know who. My husband was lying on the floor on one side to facilitate his vomiting. My children and I, bewildered, were repeatedly saying, "Oh, Lord, what is going on?" In need to be baptized of thee, and comest thou to me? And Jesus answering said unto him, Suffer it to be so now: for thus it becometh us to fulfil all righteousness. Then he suffered him. And Jesus, when he was baptized, went up straightway out of the water: and, lo, the heavens were opened unto him, and he saw the Spirit of God descending like a dove, and lighting upon him: And lo a voice from heaven, saying, This is my beloved Son, in whom I am well pleased.

Matthew 3: 13–17

At the Jordan River

Upon arrival, we found many people being baptized. Although we all had already been baptized by immersion, we decided to take a dive in the Jordan River in order to rededicate our lives to the Lord. It seemed to us that no one was allowed to go into the water with his/her own clothes or bathing suit. The awesome character of the whole place commanded it, I guess. We hired white robes at the site to go into the water. My husband, Diyenat, Capucine, and I went into the changing rooms to put on our white robes. Then, we came out, ready for the water reconsecration. Eunice and Maud were busy taking pictures and shooting this unique moment of our lives to immortalize it.

Pascal led the way. He went first into the water and dipped himself. We watched him coming up to see how he was after rededicating his life to the Lord and to read on his face what the experience meant to him. He looked happy. Then he called me. I carefully went down the few steps into the water. With his right hand on my head, he immersed me in the river. Immersing into the water and emerging gave me the glorious feeling of dying with Christ and rising up again with him. I was thrilled. I felt new. What an experience it was! Then Capucine followed suit.

> inclosed a great multitude of fishes: and their net brake. And they beckoned unto their partners, which were in the other ship, that they should come and help them. And they came, and filled both the ships, so that they began to sink. When Simon Peter saw it, he fell down at Jesus' knees, saying, Depart from me; for I am a sinful man, O Lord.
>
> Luke 5:1–8

All the experiences, miracles, and places mentioned in the Bible became reality to us. We felt privileged and honored to be in the Holy Land and experience the presence of the Lord there.

In our guided tour, there was provision for an overnight in Galilee at Astoria Hotel, before continuing toward Jerusalem. In that hotel, on the night of twenty-second breaking twenty-third of December, I had a dream. In the dream, I heard a voice telling me: "Leontine, you have not yet started preparing your songs of praise. You have only one day and a half left." The next morning, around the family breakfast table, I related this dream to my husband and our daughters. I told them I did not understand "the songs of praise" the Lord was talking about. Did he mean we had to prepare Christmas songs for the Christmas Eve? I indicated to them that I remembered the Christmas carols we just had at the office through our UNICTR Christian Fellowship. Since the following day was December 24, Christmas Eve, they suggested that I prepare a time of celebration for the family, as I usually did, with the Christmas songs that we had sang at UNICTR. I agreed.

That morning of December 23, 2010, Isaac took us to visit various Christian sites until 3:00 p.m after stopping at some restaurant, St. Peter's Fish Restaurant, for lunch. The next site was the Jordan River, the well-known river where John the Baptist baptized Jesus Christ.

> Then cometh Jesus from Galilee to Jordan unto John, to be baptized of him. But John forbad him, saying, I have

THE DIP IN THE JORDAN RIVER

On December 22, early in the morning, our guide, a friendly and knowledgeable middle-aged named Isaac, came to pick us on board a comfortable four-wheel drive assigned to the six of us. Off we went. The guided tour started. We were privileged to walk in the cities and the places mentioned in the Bible. We went to see the location the Lord transformed the water into wine. We walked in Nazareth and Capernaum, the birth place of Mary Magdala. We went to Mount Olives, where the Lord spoke the beatitudes. We had a boat ride on the Sea of Galilee. We went to the sea where Peter was fishing and he did not catch any fish until the Lord called and told him to cast his net into the deep to his right hand side and he caught a lot of fish.

> And it came to pass, that, as the people pressed upon him to hear the word of God, he stood by the lake of Gennesaret. And saw two ships standing by the lake: but the fishermen were gone out of them, and were washing their nets. And he entered into one of the ships, which was Simon's, and prayed him that he would thrust out a little from the land. And he sat down, and taught the people out of the ship. Now when he had left speaking, he said unto Simon, Launch out into the deep, and let down your nets for a draught. And Simon answering said unto him, Master, we have toiled all the night, and have taken nothing: nevertheless at thy word I will let down the net. And when they had this done, they

He had made her understand that we would remember that trip as a family and that the trip was as important as the covenant we had with Him. Indeed, as I indicated earlier on, we made a covenant with God on August 30, 1998, the terms of which are well described in my book *God Watches over Us: My Living Testimonies*. We thanked the Lord once more for the opportunity he had given us to be together for the guided tour of the Holy Land. It was a wonderful time of sharing as a family. We were totally unaware of what the Lord had in store for us!

We surrendered to God our emotions, our expectations and our walk with Him and prayed that He would make us sensitive to His voice.

We read Numbers 13:30:

> And Caleb stilled the people before Moses, and said, "Let us go up at once, and possess it; for we are well able to overcome it ", and told the Lord that with the same spirit of Caleb, we were going to possess whatever He had brought us to the Holy Land to possess.

We lifted our personal needs to God on the strength of Psalm 20:1–4

> The Lord hear thee in the day of trouble; the name of the God of Jacob defend thee; Send thee help from the sanctuary, and strengthen thee out of Zion; Remember all thy offerings, and accept thy burnt sacrifice; Selah. Grant thee according to thine own heart, and fulfil all thy counsel.

We went into intercession using Ezekiel 22:30: "And I sought for a man among them, that should make up the hedge, and stand in the gap before me for the land, that I should not destroy it: but I found none."

When we finished thanking God for the time spent in his presence, our daughter Maud shared with us what the Lord had revealed to her a couple of weeks before the trip and had given her the biblical passage of Isaiah 43:18–19:

> Remember ye not the former things, neither consider the things of old. Behold, I will do a new thing; now it shall spring forth; shall ye not know it? I will even make a way in the wilderness, and rivers in the desert.

- Purpose of family trip to the Holy Land: individual destiny, family destiny, time of refreshing, and time of reaching new level with God. Our daughters were to take this seriously, and we all were to make sure that nothing in our attitude and thoughts would prevent that purpose from being fulfilled;
- Cost of trip was high (twelve thousand dollars), but it was worthwhile. We wished to make the most of it, and we encouraged them to take care of one another during this trip through the Bible in order to allow God to speak to us. None of us was going to constitute an obstacle to what the Lord was going to do in our individual lives and in our lives as a family;
- We their parents had been married for a long time and had done everything humanly possible to care for them. Now we wished to focus on our spiritual destiny, according to the prophecy we had received from a prophet from Iceland and confirmed on three different occasions—the Lord had said that we were now called Abraham and Sarah and that he would give us many spiritual children. We needed their spiritual support in this;
- Children as a heritage from the Lord—we reiterated to them that we loved them and that they were blessed and favored by God, that whatever the Lord had said to us about each one of them had come to pass, and we reminded each one of them of what the Lord had said and done concerning them.

After this sharing, we went into a time of prayer.

We confessed our sins before the Lord and forgave one another on the basis of James 4:6–7:

> But he giveth more grace. Wherefore he saith, God resisteth the proud, but giveth grace unto the humble. Submit yourselves therefore to God. Resist the devil, and he will flee from you".

We left our rooms and went down for dinner in the hotel restaurant. Downstairs, we were to meet for the first time two staffs from Vered H. Tour, namely Charity—a Kenyan who happened to be in Tel Aviv at the same time and whom I was looking forward to seeing—and one of her colleagues, an Israeli citizen named Harel. Charity was actually the manager of Vered H. Tour branch in Nairobi. She had a room in the same hotel. We met in the lobby of the hotel and introduced ourselves. We chatted a while. Harel left. After a few minutes, we all went for dinner and sat around the same long table. Charity was nice and friendly. She shared a few things with us about her job and a few places in Israel, where she had been coming to several times a year to conduct guided tours for the benefit of her clients from Kenya. The conversation was free. Charity quickly became our friend.

When later we regained our rooms, my husband indicated his intention to have a family prayer session the same night to thank God for the family reunion and entrust into his hands the guided tour of the Holy Land we were to start the next day at 8:00 a.m. We started the prayer session with praise and worship unto the Lord and lifted our voices to express our hearts to God in thanksgiving and prayer. My husband read the Bible verse that constitutes the basis of the covenant that we as a family had concluded with God on August 30, 1998:

> But this shall be the covenant that I will make with the house of Israel; After those days, saith the Lord, I will put my law in their inward parts, and write it in their hearts; and will be their God, and they shall be my people.
>
> Jeremiah 31:33

He shared with us his heart concerning this covenant, and we both spoke to our children concerning the following:

Ireland, where she had been working, was to land an hour later. We were taken to the arrival area to wait.

The airport was busy despite the early hours. Eunice's flight landed on time, but as she could not find her luggage, she had to report the missing bag and, as a result, came out pretty late. We therefore stayed at the airport until 5:00 a.m. Then an arranged taxi took us to Metropolitan Hotel, where our rooms had been booked by the tour company. After checking in, the four of us decided to rest. On December 21, 2010, Pascal woke up early to prepare the gifts he wanted to give to his daughters—a CD containing the Word of God, mostly those Bible verses spoken by Jesus. He prepared five of them, including one for me.

Immediately after, early afternoon, Diyenat, Pascal, and I went for a tour of Tel Aviv, while Eunice stayed in the hotel as she was to receive from her employer some assignments to work on and submit online. We visited the art museum, the beach, the observatory and the diamond center. Later in the afternoon, at the lobby of the hotel, we met Isaac, our driver and guide, who came to introduce himself to us and brief us on the arrangements made for the whole visit. Afterward, we went back to the airport to meet our third daughter, Maud, arriving from Hartford, Connecticut, where she had been working. Later in the evening, we returned to Ben Gurion Airport to meet our last-born, Capucine, nicknamed Cap, short name for Capucine or Captain (Cap had been captain of the basketball team of her boarding school in Lugano, Montagnola, Switzerland, for four consecutive years before joining Liberty University in Lynchburg, Virginia). Cap was coming from her university, where she was a graduate student.

When the whole family was gathered, we had a wonderful time, conversing, catching up on the latest in our lives, bursting into laughter from time to time. We shared collective and individual moments of joy as well as of challenges. We counted the benefits of the Lord one by one and praised him for his goodness and mercy. The atmosphere was joyful and warm. We were happy together.

Kate Aboagye in 2005. I hosted them. My husband and I have known this couple for many years. They trained us and the other members of the Executive Committee of the Family Life Ministry, along with the then Senior Pastor Ken and Joy Kimiwye, Mary and Kirabo Lukwago, and the Gacanjas. They taught us the basics of marriage, counseling, family seasons, communication, and conflict resolution. They have been our main hosts in Nairobi, with our brother and countryman Jeannot Ngoma. I always thank the Lord for their warm hospitality and generosity. May the Lord richly reward them and bless their children!

On our way to Jomo Kenyatta airport on the travel day, we were to meet our pastor, Charles Akwera, of Dominion Restoration Church in Arusha, and our beloved sister Edith and her husband, Kenneth, good friends of ours and also elders in the church. They had also come to Nairobi for the weekend. We had planned to go and visit the premises of a newly planted branch of our church. We could not make it, unfortunately, because of the heavy traffic in the city of Nairobi. We therefore decided to meet directly at the airport. We arrived there just on time to pray together and say good-bye. In a corner, before we entered the check-in hall, the pastor prayed for God to give us favor and cover our trip with the blood of Jesus.

Pascal, Diyenat, and I were full of joy and expectations when we left for Israel. As a family, we had been looking forward to seeing the Holy Land and walking in the footsteps of our Lord Jesus Christ. We reached Tel Aviv, the capital city of Israel, in the early morning of December 21, 2010, around 2:00 a.m. The Israeli travel agency, Vered Hasharon Tour, the address of which I had obtained through the Embassy of Israel in Nairobi, had contacted me for the arrangements for our guided tour. It was managed by Danny, assisted by a dynamic team, including Charity in Nairobi, with whom I communicated extensively for the purpose of our trip to Israel. Vered H. Tour had sent two people to meet us at the airport upon arrival, at a location immediately after the immigration counter. The flight of our daughter Eunice, arriving from Dublin, something with us. She said she had fasted and prayed to seek God's direction in something she was believing God for—obtain school fees for an MBA program. She said, "Mum, while I was praying, I got a revelation from God I would like to share with you. The Lord revealed to me a number of things about each one of us in the family." "What did he say?" my husband and I inquired.

She indicated she had a message for each one of her sisters, for herself, as well as for her father and me. May I share with you what she said about her father, my husband, as the testimony concerns him mostly? She said the Lord told her, "I am going to make your dad a new man." And then she saw her dad in a vision, preaching to a crowd, laying hands on people, and people were getting healed. And she said, "Mum, I didn't understand that vision. However, it came to me so vividly!"

My husband and I were listening to her and following her on Skype as she was talking and demonstrating with her hands what she saw. I cracked a joke by asking my husband, "Are you going to be born again or what? You mean you are not yet born again? God said he is going to make you a new man." We both burst into laughter as we all knew he had been saved more than thirty years back. Then we thanked God for what we heard. We advised Eunice to disclose to her sisters what the Lord had revealed to her about them, and she agreed.

On December 18, 2010, Pascal and I and our daughter Diyenat, who had started working with the International Organization for Migration (IOM) in Moshi, left Arusha, Tanzania, on board an Impala bus for Nairobi, in Kenya. We were to catch our flight there on December 20, an Ethiopian Airlines aircraft to Addis Ababa and then a connecting flight to Tel Aviv. On the bus, we met our sister in Christ, Monica Odede, also a member of the UNICTR Christian Fellowship, with whom we had a chat along the way.

In Nairobi, we spent two nights at the residence of our dearest friends and spiritual leaders, David and Jayne Mutiga, and their two children, Sheila and Brian, today university graduates. I met this family for the first time at a Family Life seminar organized in Arusha by Sister students and a teacher. The election of the bureau ran simply and smoothly, just as the Lord had predicted.

The youth bureau is a welcome support to the executive committee which organizes also the seminars intended for the youths. The objective of the ministry is to bring youth to the knowledge of Christ, enable them to grow in faith and in their daily walk with God, as well as prepare them for their family, professional and social lives. My husband and I meet regularly in our home with the bureau members to share the Word, pray, praise the Lord, and train them in leadership. To date, three major youth seminars have been organized to teach them life skills and instill in them the fear of God in order to make them examples within their families, communities, and even countries. Large numbers of young men and women usually attend.

Before we took the trip, my husband and I, like many other members of the UNICTR Christian Fellowship, participated in the preparations and unfolding of Christmas carols on December 8, 2010. As was the case every year during the Christmas carols celebration, in my capacity as praise-and-worship leader of the fellowship, I led the songs sung by the fellowship and by the public during the carols. At our local church, Dominion Restoration Church, the praise-and-worship team, of which I was a member, as well as the choir, organized a special dinner for the launching of the first CD of the choir on December 16, 2010, and celebrated the birthday of the church on December 17. My husband and I were actively involved in the preparations, such as the design and printing of invitation cards, the identification and selection of the catering and decoration services, the design of the menu card, the drafting of program, the choice and practice of songs to be sung, as well as the sale of entry tickets.

On the Way to Israel

A week before we took the trip to Tel Aviv, our daughter Eunice, who was working in Dublin, Ireland, at the time, called us on Skype to share

The main speakers at these seminars are men and women of God who are knowledgeable in family matters and counseling and rich in experience. These are mainly Deputy Bishop Ken Kimiywe and his wife, Joy, in the Nairobi Pentecostal Church Valley Road; David and Jayne Mutiga, engineer and associate professor at the University of Nairobi respectively; Kirabo and Mary Lukwago, proprietors of the New Day Gospel Bookshop in Nairobi; the Bensons; David and Margaret Gacanja, marriage counselors in Nairobi, Kenya. The executive committee of the Family Life, of which my husband and I are the leaders, is made up of the following persons: Pastors Randolph and Evelyn Tebbs, Pastor Stephen and Mary Owino, Jennifer Karegyesa, Pastor Robert and his spouse Christine, Pastor Philip and his spouse, and Pastor Mayunga and his spouse. I usually play the role of master of ceremony during the seminars.

The second ministry, the Youth Ministry in Arusha, which the Lord revealed to me through his Word on May 22, 2010, during a mission in Kigali, Rwanda, started with a small seminar organized for unmarried boys and girls in Arusha on the topic "Grooming Self for Marriage." Prompted by the spirit of God, I had a heavy burden to organize this seminar with the help and participation of the abovementioned executive committee members and other Christians who were willing to join hands with my husband and I. Three hundred youths, exactly the sitting capacity of the sanctuary of the Arusha Community Church that we had hired for the occasion, honored the invitation. My husband and I covered the related organizational expenses! It rained that day! Not in the neighborhood where we were, but only on the roof and compound of the Arusha Community Church where the seminar was taking place. This is how the Youth Ministry began in Arusha.

At the time of writing, the ministry is headed by a youth bureau elected by all the participants during the last seminar held on March 31, 2012. It is composed of five young men and women as follows: a president (Joshua), a vice president (Lilian), a secretary (Glory), a deputy secretary (Stephen), and a prayer coordinator (Thomas), essentially families: Irma and Gloria Adjete, Margaret Mwaura, Doreen Maina, Pastors Evelyn and Randolph Tebbs, Debra Tulcidas, Alphonse and Rachel Van, Forias and Renifa Madenga, Moses (of late) and Esther Mutwaliza, Arlette Bikok and Pastor Mayunga, among others, and ourselves, the Mabikas. The said families are from Kenya, Togo, USA, Liberia, Tanzania, Zimbabwe, Cote d'Ivoire, Cameroon, and Congo-Brazzaville. Three of them have relocated. We would meet at our home on Thursday evenings. We would render to God powerful praise-and-worship sessions, thanksgivings, shared the Word of God, prayed and fasted for our nations, our churches, our employers, families, relatives, friends and the Saints.

We still do the same. The Lord has performed many miracles in our midst and answered innumerable prayers. These families are prayer partners and have mutually edified and supported one another. How I thank the Lord for them.

Furthermore, the Lord has granted my husband and I a burden for two other ministries for which we are coordinators in Arusha—the Family Life Ministry and the Youth Ministry in the city of Arusha. The Family Life Ministry started as a branch in Arusha at the initiative of a Ghanaian couple Alex and Kate Aboagye. When the couple relocated to the Hague, Netherlands, for professional reasons, they entrusted its coordination to my husband and me.

The Family Life Ministry sets out to build and strengthen the family unit, through national and international seminars organized annually by its executive committee on topics dealing with life within the couple, parenting, parent-child relations, celibacy, marriage and divorce, widowhood, and managing a home financially—all based on the Word of God and its principles. We believe that strong families make strong churches; strong churches, strong communities; and strong communities, strong nations. About two hundred people attend these seminars. They come from Kenya, Uganda, Rwanda, Burundi, Democratic Republic of Congo, Tanzania, the Netherlands, as well as from the United Nations community.

(UNICTR), based in Arusha, Tanzania. The UNICTR Christian Fellowship is made up of Christians from various denominations belonging to UNICTR, the East African Community (EAC), and the local churches in Arusha. The fellowship nurtures its members through sermons, Bible studies, prayer, and fasting sessions. It organizes prayers for the authorities and the country of Tanzania and other countries, the senior officials of international organizations, especially UNICTR and EAC. It undertakes visits to orphanages and juvenile prisons, where the fellowship members minister and organize Christmas carols, which are usually attended by UNICTR senior officials, staff members and their families, as well as other invited guests.

The fellowship was founded in 1996 by John Shumbusho, a Rwandan UN staff member, today a bishop of Zion City Church in Arusha, next to his God-fearing spouse, Apostle Trice Shumbusho, to whom the Lord gave the vision for the said church. The fellowship is known within the UNICTR and in the local community. The current coordinator is Randolph Tebbs, also a UN Staff from Liberia and a pastor, supported in this noble task by his spouse, Pastor Evelyn Tebbs.

I have been spiritually fed and blessed through my involvement in the UNICTR Christian Fellowship. Within the executive committee of the fellowship, I am in charge of the praise and worship. The other members are Bishop John, the coordinator of the fellowship, the spiritual adviser, the secretary, the treasurer, and their deputies. The executive committee members had been for a time the following: Pastor Shumbusho, Pastor Tebbs, Kate Aboagye, Anastasia Kamande, Irma Adjete, Pastor Moses Mutaasa, Tolu Olowoye, Debra Tulcidas, Gaudence Mukakigeli, Christine Ndahura, Feza Ramazani, Stella Karumuna, Jennifer Kahurananga and me.

For the past eleven years, my husband and I have been hosting in our home a prayer group that the Lord inspired me to start in Arusha in 2002. At the beginning, we were only a two-women meeting—me and Margaret Mwaura, a Kenyan colleague from the UNICTR. Today, the home fellowship has grown to include, among others, the following

THE REVELATION

Background

At the time of writing, my husband and I have been married for thirty-three years. Praise be to God! God has given us an inheritance—four marvelous daughters aged from thirty-two to twenty-seven years. Their names are Eunice, Diyenat Sandie, Maud, and Capucine. My husband and I have done, and continue to do, our best to train them in the way they ought to go. And as they grow in life, we have reasons to believe that they have not departed from it, as you will also realize from the facts below. "Train up a child in the way he should go: and when he is old, he will not depart from it" (Prov 22:6).

For the past sixteen years, our daughters have been studying and working abroad, especially in the United States of America, Ireland, England, and Trinidad and Tobago. My husband and I have been living alone, seeing them whenever possible. In 2010, we had not spent Christmas together for ten years. They would be together somewhere and we in Africa. This was why as a family we made a decision to spend Christmas together in Israel and seize that opportunity to visit the Holy Land. For a long time, my husband had wanted us to meet there as a family so that we could pray and discover Israel together. The said visit was to take place from December 22 to 30, 2010. We all made the necessary plans a year in advance. Since we lived in different countries, we decided to meet in Tel Aviv.

My husband and I are members of a Christian fellowship within our office, the United Nations International Criminal Tribunal for Rwanda

Israel, who stood with us in prayer during this particular trying time and also for posterity, I wish to thank you all from the bottom of my heart for your work of love in God's service. Kindly remember that your work in the Lord will not be in vain and that the Lord is the rewarder of all things. "The liberal soul shall be made fat: and he that watereth shall be watered also himself" (Prov 11:25).

I wish also to declare that the God that we all serve is alive. The Bible says: "Praise ye the LORD. O give thanks unto the LORD; for he is good: for his mercy endureth for ever;" (Ps 106:1).

Here is the story.

INTRODUCTION

There is nothing else I have to do, nothing else I can do, but to give a testimony, before God himself and before men. In obedience to the Word of God, I am giving the said testimony on behalf of my family and on my own behalf, in thanksgiving to our Father in heaven, the Almighty God: "But thanks be to God, which giveth us the victory through our Lord Jesus Christ" (1 Cor 15:57).

According to the Bible, the testimony is to be given at home to family members and neighbor and friends, as in Mark 5:19: "Howbeit Jesus suffered him not, but saith unto him, Go home to thy friends, and tell them how great things the Lord hath done for thee, and hath had compassion on thee." as well as to the body of Christ in the assembly of the saints as in Ephesians 5:19–20:

> [19]Speaking to yourselves in psalms and hymns and spiritual songs, singing and making melody in your heart to the Lord;

> [20]Giving thanks always for all things unto God and the Father in the name of our Lord Jesus Christ;

I am putting this unique experience in writing for the earthly and heavenly record. For my husband and our daughters; for the Dominion Restoration Church and the people of God in Arusha, Tanzania; for my relatives, friends, partners, men and women of God in Kenya, Congo-Brazzaville, Cameroon, France, Ireland, United States of America, and someone who could take dictation and type fast. This was how the first drafts of two manuscripts were written. The first one was written by my husband about his miracle experience in Israel, where he had fallen in a coma for twelve days while on vacation with myself and our four daughters and was brought back to life with a message from the Lord. He dictated this message to a Beninese student introduced to us by my sister-in-law, Josephine, and the latter typed it. The other manuscript was typed, under my dictation, by my daughter Capucine, who was then reading for an MBA at Liberty University in Virginia, USA. It happened that just at that moment she had a few days off and wanted to come to visit us in France for six days.

The third manuscript, given as a testimony at a church in Arusha, Tanzania, was to be typed and proofread. It tells the story of the victory the Lord gave my daughters and me after much prayer while in Israel to visit the Holy Land through a unique experience. My husband, Pascal Mabika, unexpectedly had a brain hemorrhage due to an aneurysm that burst out immediately after he came out of the Jordan River, where he had dipped himself to rededicate his life to the Lord along with Capucine and me. He was rushed to the hospital in Haifa on December 23, 2010 in the night and underwent neurosurgery in the head on twenty-fourth of December. He fell into a coma. Miraculously, God brought him back to life after twelve days—with a message.

PREFACE

This book is one of the three books the Lord showed to me in a vision in the second or third night of October 2011 in Tours, France, while I was on sick leave in the residence of my elder sister and her husband, Delphine and Daphtone Mbouyou, respectively retired bank manager and neurosurgeon. The sick leave was the result of a neurosurgery I underwent in the lower part of my back to remove a cyst that had grown due to a rough fall on the back five years earlier while playing volleyball with my office team. As I had indicated in my other book entitled *God Watches over Us: My Living Testimonies*, the surgery took place on the twenty-sixth of September 2011 and I was discharged on the thirtieth. The neurosurgeon who operated me instructed me not to undertake any trip before three weeks.

Around second to third October, in the middle of the night, I felt someone waking me up softly by touching my shoulder while my husband was fast asleep beside me. I tried to open my eyes in the dark in an attempt to figure out what was happening. And I heard a voice telling me as in a reprimand, "You could have done something all the time you have been here. You could have written three books. It is not for nothing that I have extended your stay here!" As the voice spoke, I saw clearly the three books with titles, chapters, and some writings passing before my eyes as in a dream and how they would be written—one was by my husband in French and two by me in English. I woke up abruptly and woke up my husband to share that "dream vision."

My husband was supportive. We prayed about it and decided to obey. With that burden, the next morning, I started looking for

    God's Miracle 62
    Out of the Intensive Care Unit 66
    Arrangements for Medical Evacuation 68
On the Eagle Wings 74
    Medical Evacuation to Tours, France 74
    On Board Flight El Alal 75
    Admission in Hopital Bretonneau (Tours) 77
    Life in the House and Rehabilitation Exercises 80
New Skin 84
    Return to Arusha 84
    Thanksgiving to the Lord 86
What an Experience! 94
    Individual Experiences of Our Four Daughters 94
Conclusion 101

CONTENTS

Preface 1
Introduction 3
The Revelation 5
    Background 5
    On the Way to Israel 9
The Dip in the Jordan River 17
    At the Jordan River 19
    At Poriya Medical Center 21
The Long Night 24
    Transfer to Rambam Medical Center in Haifa 24
    In the Intensive Care Unit 26
God With Me 28
    Move to the Surgery Rooms 28
    In the Surgery Rooms 31
    At the Basement of the Hospital 36
    Back to Intensive Care Unit 39
    In the City of Haifa 41
The Dark Valley With a Glimpse of Light 45
    The Coma 45
    Seeking God's Intervention 48
    God's Directions 55
    The Battle of Faith 58
The Miracle 62

FROM THE JORDAN RIVER TO HIS BEDSIDE

LEONTINE BIRANGUI MABIKA

www.ingramcontent.com/pod-product-compliance
Lightning Source LLC
Chambersburg PA
CBHW041324110526
44592CB00021B/2812